The Alcuin Club
and its Publications
1897 – 1987

An Annotated Bibliography

Peter J. Jagger

Second Edition

AN ALCUIN PUBLICATION

Published on behalf of the Alcuin Club by
Hymns Ancient & Modern Ltd, St Marys Works,
St Mary's Plain, Norwich, Norfolk NR3 3BH

Printed by BPCC Northern Printers Ltd., Stanley Road, Bllackpool FY1 4QN
Member of The BPCC Group

CONTENTS

In 1975 the Revd Peter Jagger, now Warden of St Deiniol's Library, Hawarden, did the Alcuin Club a noteworthy service by compiling an Annotated Bibliography of the Club's publications from 1897 to 1974*. It was felt by the Committee that it would be appropriate to bring this work up to date, to mark the Club's 90th anniversary in 1987. Unfortunately pressure of academic work made it impossible for Mr Jagger to undertake it. Dr Geoffrey Cuming kindly agreed to bring the bibliography up to date, while Archdeacon Timms, Chairman of the Club, was asked to supplement Mr Jagger's historical introduction.

---

*An abridgement of the Alcuin Lecture for 1974: delivered by the Reverend Peter J. Jagger, M.A., at the Annual General Meeting of the Alcuin Club in St Andrew's Courthouse, Holborn, London, on Wednesday, June 26th, 1974.

The Lecture was based almost entirely upon the unpublished records of the Alcuin Committee: minute books, correspondence, and various miscellaneous documents, covering the first 77 years of the Club's existence.

PART I

THE HISTORY OF
THE ALCUIN CLUB
Some Insights into Liturgical Study, Writing, and Publishing

A. THE BACKGROUND AND BIRTH OF THE ALCUIN CLUB

1. The Age of Societies

On January 12th, 1897 four Anglican laymen met together and resolved that: 'A Club to be called the Alcuin Club be and is hereby constituted.' In *The Alcuin Club and Its Publications: 1897–1972*, I wrote: 'The Alcuin Club is unique in its existence and in the number and range of its scholarly publications.' In saying this I did not mean that there were no other nineteenth-century Clubs and Societies with ecclesiastical and liturgical interests. The nineteenth century witnessed the formation of numerous ecclesiastical Clubs e.g., the Bannatyne Club, the Caxton Society, the English Historical Society, the Wycliffe Society, the Camden Society, to name but a few. Perhaps the Alcuin Club has the most in common with the now non-existent Camden Society, which was formed in 1839. Members of the Camden Society soon came to realize that it was impossible to understand the function of the Medieval Church without diligent research into service-books, visitation articles, parochial records and the devotional and dogmatic writings of the Middle Ages. Their study of the vestments and ornaments of the Church led them to a careful examination of monumental brasses and illuminated manuscripts, in addition to the usual written sources. The sources used, and the publications produced by the Camden Society, reveal a close affinity to the early period of the Alcuin Club. In 1848 the Camden Society became the Ecclesiological Society, a Society that did much to stimulate interest in traditional Catholic worship and thus made its contribution towards the liturgical and ceremonial revival of the 19th century.

In view of the rather short life of the Camden Society and the existence of numerous other ecclesiastical Clubs and Societies, could the formation of yet another Club be justified? The early Alcuin Committee sincerely believed so, and in the end-pages of their first publications offered a kind of rationale for the Club's formation and existence.

The wisdom of the Founder Members and the justification of their action is seen in the fact that the Club has outlived many of its contemporaries which are now no more than largely forgotten Victorian ecclesiastical Clubs and Societies which bore rather grand titles.

Whilst the existence of the Alcuin Club can be partly attributed to the vogue of the period in which it came into being, there were other factors which were primarily responsible for its genesis: namely the growing interest in and practical study of ceremonial, church furniture, and ornaments, upon English lines, and the conviction that there must be strict obedience to the Prayer Book. Historic research was to be the foundation of all Alcuin publications on these subjects, but in the 19th century some of these subjects were the cause of deep and bitter conflict and controversy.

2. The Age of Conflict and Controversy

The Alcuin Club was born in a period of ecclesiastical conflict and controversy over liturgical and ceremonial issues. While Pusey and the loyal Tractarians disclaimed any connection with the ritualists and emphasized loyalty to the Prayer Book, it was, nevertheless, their high doctrine of the Sacraments which inspired the increasing use of ceremonial. Tractarian uneasiness about ritualism and their adamant rejection of ceremonial usage could not remove the logical development of the situation: when men embraced Catholic doctrine, emphasizing the Eucharist and the Real Presence, it was somewhat natural that they would wish to express that faith in the forms of worship and ceremony used by the Catholic Church down through the centuries, and so the conflict and controversy over ceremonial issues continued.

In the 1860s and early 1870s many pamphlets were published in connection with the ritual controversies of the period. The period witnessed a growing support of ceremonial amongst both clergy and laity. But this did not prevent the Judicial Committee of the Privy Council pronouncing in 1871 the illegality of Eucharistic Vestments, the Eastward Position, the Mixed Chalice and the use of Wafer Bread. The Lincoln Judgement of 1890 marks a very real stage in the liturgical and ceremonial life of the Church of England. Bishop Edward King was charged with the illegal use of various ceremonial practices. Archbishop Benson allowed all the points of issue to be re-examined, after which the only point pronounced illegal was the use of the sign of the cross. The Lincoln Judgement shows that in the light of greater liturgical knowledge, earlier Judgements on liturgical matters can be re-examined and, if necessary, changed; the epoch of ritual persecution was now over and diocesan bishops were usually left to decide upon such issues. Persecutions may have ended, but not interest in liturgiology and ceremonial practice.

During this period of ritual controversy, pressure for the Revision of the Prayer Book also provoked numerous pamphlets, sermons, public meetings and petitions to Parliament, but liturgical improvement was not amongst the many reasons put forward for Prayer Book Revision. Such was the background and setting in which the Alcuin Club came into being in 1897.

3. The Founder Members

The first Minute Book records the names of the four founder members of the Club: Dr J. Wickham Legg, H. B. Briggs, W. H. St John Hope, and J. T. Micklethwaite, all of them Anglican laymen. The Minute Book records the resolutions of the first meeting, but unfortunately nothing is recorded of the discussion which lay behind the resolutions. The consitution of the Club, its objectives, and the conditions of membership were all decided upon by these four laymen. Eleven gentlemen were invited to attend their next meeting; amongst these eleven were seven clergymen, including Brightman, Frere, Wilson, and Wordsworth.

Looking back, the lay origin of the Alcuin Club may seem a little surprising; perhaps it was, but the 19th century witnessed a growing interest amongst Anglican laity in things liturgical, ceremonial, and doctrinal. In 1867 a layman, Montagu Burrows, wrote of the growing interest of the laity in ecclesiastical matters, Church government, worship, and doctrine. He saw this interest as an attempt, by the laity, to obtain a real foothold within the life of the Church of England. The *Church Times* of May 1876 stated: 'We have constantly pointed out that the so-called ritualist phase of the Catholic revival is due to the laity far more than to the clergy.' Twenty years later the four lay Founder Members of the Alcuin Club bear witness to the increased interest amongst the laity in matters of worship, ceremonial, and doctrine.

B. THE CLUB'S OBJECTIVES AND ACHIEVEMENTS

It was the Club's four lay founders, and not the more expert clerical members of the Committee, who fixed the Club's Object and Work. At their first meeting these four laymen resolved that: 'The object of the said Club be to promote the study of the history and use of the Book of Common Prayer.' The Prayer Book was to be central in all the Club's activities and the 'touch-stone' and guiding principle of all its publications. The Anglican ethos of the Club was further emphasized by restricting membership to those in communion with the Church of England.

The four laymen also resolved that: 'The work of the Club be the publication of Tracts dealing with the Object of the Club, and such other works as may seem desirable, with reproductions of miniatures from MSS and photographs of Church Furniture, Ornaments and Vestments.' One could sum up both the Object and Work of the Club as the fostering of liturgical study and publication of liturgical works which have some connection with the Book of Common Prayer. During its 90-year history the Club has in fact issued over 150 liturgical publications, which may be divided into six main groups.

1. The Collections

From the outset the Club's major publications, now 68 in number, have been described as Collections, and these have established the Club's international reputation for sound liturgical scholarship. These works cover a wide range of subjects and offer an unrivalled source of liturgical information. The many and varied subjects covered by the Collections show how the Object and Work of the Club have been broadly interpreted. Occasionally some members of the Committee have felt that their publications were going beyond the avowed aims of the Club, and the Minute Books reveal how a number of the Collections were the cause of much heated conflict, and also a source of financial embarrasment which, it was felt, inhibited the Club's wider work and influence.

7

2. The Tracts

The so-called Tracts, i.e. smaller books, make up the second group of 36 publications, many of which reflected the interests and controversies of the period in which they were written and published. On the whole, the Tracts contain some valuable liturgical material and have helped to clarify the liturgical ideas and ceremonial practices of many Anglican clergymen. Amongst the Tracts are the Club's two 'best-sellers', *A Directory of Ceremonial* and *A Server's Manual;* both went into several editions and sold many thousands of copies.

3. The Pamphlets

At a Committee Meeting on July 8th, 1910, it was reported that the Club was in grave financial difficulty, but this did not prevent the Chairman suggesting that in view of the move for the Revision of the Prayer Book, the time had come for a group of liturgical experts to indicate what really ought to be done, and he wondered if the Club would be justified in attempting this. Two weeks later they discussed Prayer Book Revision and agreed to invite various liturgical scholars to write on the subject; what they wrote was to be printed as one tract without the names of the contributors. It was hoped that such a tract would sell well and make a substantial profit for the Club. Unfortunately, those invited to undertake the work did not favour the suggested tract and mistrusted a composite production. The idea was dropped and, as an alternative, F. E. Brightman was asked to write a tract on the subject, but both this and a promised tract on Reservation failed to materialize.

Frere wrote to the Committee in December 1911 advising them to continue printing tracts on Prayer Book Revision. On February 27th, 1912 they agreed to publish a series of pamphlets on the subject, prefaced by a note explaining the position of the Committee, and so the Alcuin Pamphlets came into being. Ten years later Prayer Book Revision was felt to constitute a situation of such urgency that in October 1923 the Committee agreed to meet on a fixed day every month for the following six months. Amidst another financial crisis, caused by the publication of Kennedy's Collections on Elizabethan Episcopal Administration (xxv – xxvii), the Club produced and published pamphlets 12–14, *A Survey of the Proposals for the Alternative Prayer Book*, the so-called 'Orange Books'. A second edition of pamphlet 12 sold 400 copies in one week; and by February 1924 a total of 6,000 Orange Books had been sold. These three pamphlets undoubtedly made a valuable contribution to the Prayer Book Revision movement of that period and show how the Club faced up to a very real need during a liturgical crisis within the Church of England.

4. The Manuals

This series of short booklets concerned with the practical presentation of the liturgy began in 1978, replacing the Tracts. A second edition of the first Manual was soon called for.

5. Miscellaneous Publications

This group contains a number of publications which do not fit into the Club's three main categories of publications. Amongst these publications are the Committee's attempts to produce popular liturgical leaflets.

6. The Occasional Journals

It has long been the practice of the Club to invite a scholar to give a lecture at the Annual General Meeting. This series, which began in 1975, replaced the Pamphlets.

We are now in a position to ask and to try to answer the question of whether or not the Club has achieved the object for which it was created. Evidence suggests that it has. In spite of its failure to achieve a wider sphere of influence, due in part to its publication of a number of costly and questionable works, it has in fact published more liturgical books than any other society, and has made a valuable contribution to Prayer Book Revision and liturgical study in general. Unfortunately, apart from a few less specialized Tracts and Pamphlets, the Club's publications have never had a very wide circulation, and the failure of the attempts to popularize liturgical literature should serve as a continual reminder that liturgiology is a subject of limited appeal.

C. WRITING AND PUBLISHING

As the Club exists primarily to promote and publish scholarly liturgical works, it is not surprising that most of the Committee's Meetings and correspondence, since its foundation in 1897, have been chiefly concerned with the world of writing and publishing. The Club's records provide a remarkable, perhaps a unique insight into the difficulties and hazards of the literary world. Here we can only take a brief glimpse at a few of the recorded facts.

1. Writing

Tract 1, Ornaments of the Rubric, by J. T. Micklethwaite, was the very first Alcuin publication. Micklethwaite's manuscript was scrutinized in a way that no modern author would like to face. The minutes of the Committee's 4th meeting state: 'After consideration and making of sundry alterations the paper was agreed to, to the end of page 4'. This was on May 4th, 1897. On October 15th of that year, after six more meetings and a sentence by sentence examination of the manuscript, the Committee finally agreed to its publication. But even after such careful scrutiny an Advertisement at the time of publication stated: 'The Alcuin Club Tracts are issued under the direct supervision of the Committee, but the author of a tract, when it is published with his name, is alone responsible for its details.' The 58-page Tract contains 4 pages of sources and a six-page double-column index. Micklethwaite's labours were rewarded by a gift of 25 copies of the Tract. The way in which the Committee handled this first manuscript set something of a precedent for the future, which can be summed up under four headings.

I. The Committee decide what shall be published under the Alcuin Club imprint, and all publications must be in accord with the Object and Work of the Club.

In December, 1903 the Committee rejected a manuscript submitted to them on the grounds of its limited liturgical value, but at that same meeting they agreed to the publication of the Edwardian Inventories. When, in 1905, publication of these Inventories was nearing completion, the Committee were not sure whether they ought to be classed as Collections or Tracts. But such uncertainty did not prevent them from agreeing to publish numerous other Inventories, which over the years took up much of the Committee's time and even more of the Club's finances.

A financial crisis in 1923, and opposition from some of the Committee, nearly prevented the publication of Collections xxv – xxvii on *Elizabethan Episcopal Administration*. Frere, who had devoted much time to this work, expressed the view that while Kennedy's book would entail considerable cost, 'the Club was pledged to produce it.' A number of

11

Committee members felt that the proposed three volumes were not what was desired by present members and that the expenditure involved was not justifiable. Duncan-Jones stated: 'Due to recent publications, the Club has reached a position of importance and authority in the Church of England and the publication of a work which only remotely bears upon the principles of the Club will very seriously hamper the practical usefulness of much other work it might undertake.' His plea went unheeded, and the costly publication went ahead.

Thirty years later there was another conflict on the issue of what ought to be published. Two very scholarly members of the Committee were asked to examine a manuscript for possible publication. After examining the manuscript, they both questioned its accuracy and expressed the opinion that it was contrary to the spirit of the Prayer Book, and ran counter to Anglican authority and the declared aims and objects of the Alcuin Club. So firm were their convictions that they felt that, if the manuscript was published, they could not conscientiously allow their names to appear as members of the Committee, and thus offered their resignations. The Committee were divided on the issue. A reply to the letter of resignation stated: 'I am quite at a loss when you say that the work is contrary to the spirit of the Book of Common Prayer!' Another member expressed the view that perhaps it was inevitable that the Club should cast its net wide, but at the same time felt that the Club's publications should always have a direct connection with the Prayer Book, if it was to be loyal to its avowed purpose and principles. In the end the controversial manuscript was never published by the Club.

While the long list of Alcuin Publications shows that the net has been cast very wide, it gives no indication of the vast number of subjects, titles, and projected publications considered over the years by the Committee. W. K. Lowther Clarke expressed the view that some of the valuable suggestions made to the Committee would be most suitable subjects of theses for higher degrees and subsequent Alcuin publications, a suggestion which gained the written approval of Professor Henry Chadwick. The Minute Books also tell of many manuscripts considered but never published – what happened to these?

Occasionally the Committee were not as thorough as they ought to have been. When they accepted Cuthbert Atchley's manuscript on the Litany, eventually published as Tract 6, T. A. Lacey, a member of the Committee, reminded them that they had already asked him to write a book on the same subject.

In 1904 Dr Wickham Legg wrote to the Committee suggesting the publication of the Carthusian Rite, of which we hear no more until 1911, when Francis Eeles, a member of the Committee, found amongst his papers some galley proofs on the Carthusian Rite. It would seem that the proofs of the book had been lost for several years, and it was in fact never published.

The records reveal that there can sometimes be a very fine line drawn between the ultimate rejection or publication of a manuscript. Dearmer's *Parson's Handbook* was turned down as unsuitable, but when commercially published was so successful that it went into many editions and sold several thousand copies.

II. The Club is not averse to publishing manuscripts of a provocative nature or limited appeal.

A number of Alcuin publications have either dealt with controversial subjects or been the cause of some controversy.

Tract V, *A First Ordo*, began in 1902 as the work of an individual but, after a long and difficult passage, it was published as a composite work by 'some members of the Alcuin Club.' The minutes tell how it was produced with great caution and difficulty, and controversial points were carefully clarified. Even so, we are told that it met with 'a remarkably unfavourable reception', and 'no one spoke well of it.' Indeed, there were complaints on every side. One member of the Committee resigned, another threatened resignation. In view of this reception, the Committee, which had already announced the publication of *A Second English Ordo*, quickly dropped the idea. Some works were published in an attempt to throw light on difficult and controversial subjects, e.g., the use of Incense, Lights, Ornaments, Vestments, Reservation, to name a few.

The fact that liturgiology has never been a popular subject means that Alcuin publications have always had a rather limited appeal, but this has never deterred the Committee's work or dampened their enthusiasm. A number of publications were undertaken simply because it was felt that the manuscripts were of value to liturgical scholars and students, and thus ought to be published.

III. The Club demands sound, well-documented, scholarly works.

Manuscripts have been rejected on a number of occasions because it was felt that they did not meet the high academic standard demanded by the Club. Whilst the Committee have sometimes been willing to reconsider a manuscript after considerable amendment or in some cases complete re-writing, they have been unwilling to lower their standards. These consistently high standards, the quality of the Club's publications, plus the fact that many distinguished authors have written for the Club, have all helped to build up the Club's academic reputation.

IV. Alcuin Authors do not receive the established rates of royalties.

In 1899 W. H. St John Hope, editor of the Club's first Collections, received 12 copies of his work as a reward for his labour. Percy Dearmer, on the other hand, received £10 for Collection V and a percentage on outside sales. In 1913 the author of Pamphlet III was given £5 and made an honorary member for 5 years, while the author of *Reservation* was presented with copies of the Club's publications.

The Club's system of rewarding its authors has been somewhat unusual and varied, but Alcuin authors have never expected, and certainly never received, adequate financial reward for their work. Nevertheless, their labours have been rewarded. A letter written in 1958 by Noel Davy, editor of SPCK to Lowther Clarke, provides an illustration. Writing about an Alcuin author, Davy said: 'The author was told . . . he could expect no royalty on the first edition . . . He entirely accepted the fact that, to have a scholarly book published at this stage of his career, is a more substantial recompense for an author than the payment of an actual royalty.' There are numerous Alcuin authors who would entirely concur with that statement. However, in more recent years, the situation has changed, and there is now an agreed figure given to the author of every work accepted for publication.

2. Publishing

The major problem which the Club has had to face throughout its history is that of inadequate finance. The Club's records provide valuable insight into the world of publishing and the hazards and costs of producing literary works.

In 1899 the Committee agreed that the total cost for producing 250 copies of their first Collections be kept within £60. In 1916, 500 copies of Freestone's book on Reservation cost £101, whilst two years later 500 copies of Wyatt's pamphlet on the Burial Service cost only £12. 7s. 6d. By the 1930's high production costs were becoming a matter of grave concern for the Committee. Estimates were received in 1931 for Dunlop's 79-page Tract on Processions: 1,500 copies were to cost £51. In 1940, 1,000 copies of the Frere Memorial volume cost about £250, but in 1953 Dr Jasper's book on Frere cost £750 for only 500 copies. In 1974 the production costs for an edition of 1,000 copies were just over £2,000, eight times the cost in 1940. These figures give some indication of the phenomenal increase in the production costs of the Club's publications. Ever-increasing costs have led the Committee to change publishing houses on a number of occasions in an attempt to obtain more satisfactory terms.

D. MEMBERSHIP AND MEMBERS

1. The Conditions of Membership

After only two meetings, the condition of membership and the constitution of the Club had been decided upon. Membership subscription was to be £1, entitling members to all publications *gratis*, while Associates paid 5s, which entitled them to receive Tracts free, and other publications at a reduced rate. Members and Associates had to be elected by the Committee, and must be in communion with the Church of England. While this stipulation was removed in 1913 in order to allow membership to libraries and non-Anglicans, it did not lead to any immediate significant increase in membership, which may have been due to the outbreak of war.

2. The Need to Increase Membership

On January 25th, 1897 'the Chairman was requested to adopt such measures as he might think best for making the

Club known, and securing members.' From the outset it was realised that the success of the Club depended upon a reasonable number of paying members and, throughout the Club's history, membership and the payment of subscriptions have occupied much of the Committee's valuable time. The records offer some interesting side-lights on this subject.

After only six months the Club had secured 124 members and 31 associates. Ten years later (1907) there were 243 members and 84 associates, but not all were regular in the payment of their subscriptions. During the period 1910-12 there was an all-out attempt to collect unpaid subscriptions. Many objected to the request and resigned. Membership slumped to 150 with 70 associates. In 1932 a circular was sent out to various people inviting them to join the Club. Amongst the replies were two from notable bishops, who declined the invitation on the grounds of finance. The £1 subscription prompted Bishop Henson to write that he could not add to his financial obligations, while Bishop Kirk said that he would join when he had sorted out his finance. Gradually over the years membership began to increase once again, and by the 1950s it passed 300: by the 1960s it reached 500, and in 1974 there were nearly 800 members.

Dedicated members have always been eager to tell others of the Club's work and publications, and the records show that substantial increases in membership, at various periods in the Club's history, have been largely due to the zealous propaganda of individual committee members, for such members have realized that the continuance of the Club ultimately depends upon an adequate paid-up membership. There is little doubt that the long life and effective work of the Club has been primarily due to the zeal and dedicated work of those who have served on the Committee, men like Walter Howard Frere, Athelstan Riley, A. S. Duncan-Jones,

17

W. K. Lowther Clarke, and J. H. Arnold. One could say a great deal about these gifted faithful servants of the Club and of the secretaries, treasurers, and presidents who contributed their own special gifts. Perhaps the Club has benefited most of all from the contribution made by the many very able scholars whose wide ecclesiological and liturgical knowledge has been made available to the Club an through the Club to the Church at large.

3. The Problem of Resignations

One of the chief reasons why membership has never been high is because of continual resignations. From time to time, quite a few members have resigned when pressed to pay their arrears in subscriptions. But there have also been other reasons for resignations, such as the conflicts and controversies which have often surrounded the subject of liturgy, especially in ceremonial matters, e.g., Vestments, Incense, Lights and Reservation, to name but a few of the more obvious.

The Club's first President, George Brown, Bishop of Bristol, offered his resignation early in 1899, which was followed by the resignation of three other episcopal members. The Committee felt that the President's resignation was due to some misunderstanding concerning the Club's position. In an attempt to clarify the situation, a resolution was passed on April 20th, 1899: 'The Committee of the Alcuin Club, in accepting with regret the resignation of the presidency of the Bishop of Bristol, takes this opportunity of declaring that no member of the Club or of the Committee is to be regarded as in any way committed to any opinion expressed in the publications of the Club.'

But such clarification did not satisfy everyone. On at least two different occasions there have been resignations from the

Committee on matters of conviction. But convictions in matters liturgical and ceremonial not only caused resignations but also prevented others from joining the Club. In 1932 Lord Halifax, who had been invited to join the Club, replied to the invitation saying that he felt unable to join or offer any support. A letter from Bishop Kenneth Kirk, in 1938, replying to an invitation to become the Club's President, stated that he could not accept the invitation because of his use of modern Roman ceremonial which he felt was 'more than a good many members and publications of the Alcuin Club seem willing to allow.' He went on to say that if he became President he would find himself 'obliged continually to disassociate myself from expressions or views contained in your publications; whilst you would equally find yourselves obliged to disavow ceremonial which I habitually use'. However, having refused the office of President, he wrote a month later agreeing to become a member of the Club.

4. The Problem of Finance

The Club's two main sources of income have always been subscriptions and profits from the sale of publications. On a few occasions the Club has received private gifts which have sometimes ensured the publication of a particular manuscript. Because of its rather limited sources of income, it is not difficult to see why finance has always been one of the Club's major problems. Threats to the Club's continuity have invariably been on financial grounds, and usually because of the number or size of publications undertaken by the Committee. But having said this, it must be admitted that the Alcuin Committees of the past have never had an easy task. They have made numerous attempts to increase the Club's assets, by trying to increase the number of subscribing members, through the regular collection of subscriptions, through numerous attempts to promote greater sales and in 1960 through the formation of Alcuin Ltd.

E. FROM 1974 TO 1987

In this historical introduction to the original edition of the Alcuin bibliography, Mr Jagger makes several important points. First, how much the Club has owed to 'the zeal and dedication of those who served on the Committee'. The death of the Revd Dr W. K. Lowther Clarke in 1968 removed one who, as Chairman, guided the fortunes of the Club for thirteen years, and whose wisdom, meticulous scholarship, and experience of publishing proved invaluable in maintaining the Club's progress in the post-war years. During this time Dr Ronald Jasper was invited to serve on the Committee, and gave distinguished service as Editorial Secretary, until his translation to the Deanery of York in 1975. He was succeeded in this office by Dr Geoffrey Cuming, who in 1977 resigned owing to pressure of work, and was succeeded by Dr Paul Bradshaw, until his acceptance of a teaching post at Notre Dame University in the USA in 1985, when Dr Cuming generously agreed to reassume the office. In addition to those mentioned by Mr Jagger, other names which appear in the minutes as members of the Committee are those of Dr Jocelyn Perkins, Dr G. G. Willis, Dr Cyril Pocknee, Canon J. D. C. Fisher, Dr F. Brittain, Dr F. J. E. Raby, all of whom contributed to the Club's reputation by their scholarly contributions. Nor should our Presidents be forgotten – Dr J. W. C. Wand, one time Bishop of London; Hugh Ashdown, one time Bishop of Newcastle; Dr Eric Kemp, Bishop of Chichester.

Mr Jagger also remarks that membership and finance have

been perennial problems in the life of the Club. In no small measure this has been due to the Club's inability to pay an adequate sum for secretarial work, and this again has been due to the inadequacy of the annual subscription demanded of members. In the beginning this was established at £1.00, and so remained for half a century, until in the 1950s it was raised by one shilling to a guinea. In 1970 it became two guineas, raised later to £5.00, and recently to £7.00. Even so, when compared with the price of books in the 1980s, it seems but little, and has meant that the annual major volume could no longer be published in the traditional hard covers. Had it not been for the energetic, enthusiastic, and sustained work of Mr James Holden, appointed Membership Secretary in 1971 and subsequently also Hon. Treasurer, the membership at home and abroad would be half what it is, and the present healthy reserves of the Club non-existent.

Just what shape the future holds for the Club, we know not – but we hope, and will endeavour to see, that it will remain an honoured place in liturgical study and in service to the Church.

George Timms

PART II

THE ALCUIN COLLECTIONS
I to LXVIII

I HOPE, Sir W. H. St JOHN. English Altars: from Illuminated Manuscripts with descriptive notes. pp. 60, 14 ill., Longmans, Green; 1899.

This volume was both the first of the Alcuin Collections, and the first of a series of Alcuin publications: 'in illustration of the Ecclesiological Antiquities of the English Church, with special reference to the Ornaments of the Church, and of the Ministers thereof, at all times of their ministration.'

On fourteen large plates, $16\frac{1}{2}'' \times 13''$, we have thirty-six finely produced pictures of English Altars from the 10th to the 16th century. The pictures are reproduced from illuminated manuscripts and arranged in chronological order, each illumination being accompanied by very brief descriptive notes. Altar furnishings, fabrics, vestments, architecture, and religious symbolism during the period covered, are but some of the themes which can be traced by means of these selected illuminations.

II FRERE, WALTER HOWARD. Exposition de la Messe: from La Légende Dorée of Jean de Vignay – with illuminations. pp. 56, 10 ill., Longmans, Green; 1899.

The format of this volume is the same as Collections I. The ten illustrated pages contain twenty-two illuminations from a French version of the *Legenda Aurea* of Jacobus de Voragine. While the 15th-century manuscript, here used, was defective, in that some illustrations had not been completed, nevertheless it offers the most complete series of illuminations available and offers a valuable elucidation of the ceremonial of the Mass as performed in Northern France at the end of the 15th century. The actual Use described corresponds almost entirely with the Roman Use before the Tridentine revision. The text of the 'Exposition' is given and brief notes accompany each illumination. There are four Appendixes giving extracts from: The Lay Folk's Mass Book, the Manner and Mode of the Mass, Merita Missae, and the Displaying of the Popish Mass.

III FRERE, WALTER HOWARD. Pontifical Services: Illustrated from miniatures of the XVth and XVIth centuries, with descriptive notes and a liturgical introduction. Volume I, pp. 115, Longmans, Green; 1901.

Because of the mass of available material on the Illuminations and Services belonging to the medieval Pontificals, the Alcuin Club decided to publish two volumes on this subject under the editorship of Frere.

This first volume contains the Liturgical Introduction, examining the history of some important Pontifical Services and a summary description of English manuscript Pontificals. Volume II, Collection IV, contains a series of miniatures illustrative of the Pontifical Services. In the Liturgical Introduction Frere concentrates on Pontifical Services not in the BCP, viz: the Consecration of a Church, the Profession of a Monk, the Consecration of a Nun, the Services of a Deaconess and of a Widow. A valuable section dealing with English Pontificals in manuscript is followed by an appendix on Episcopal Ceremonies from the Lansdowne Manuscript 451, and three indexes of the Liturgical Forms.

IV FRERE, WALTER HOWARD. Pontifical Services: Illustrated from Miniatures of the XVth and XVIth centuries, with descriptive notes and a liturgical introduction. Volume II, pp. 88, including 20 plates, Longmans, Green; 1901.

This is both a unique and fascinating work. Twenty plates, giving some sixty-two reproductions, on pages $16\frac{1}{2}'' \times 13''$, illustrate various Pontifical Services of Ordination and Blessing. To name but some of the illuminations will be sufficient to indicate the breadth of the work. Ordinations of Readers, Exorcists, Acolytes, Deacons, Priests, and the Consecration and Enthronment of a Bishop. The Blessing of an Abbot, Abbess, Widow, Episcopal Insignia, Hermit and Pontifical Ornaments, Consecration of a Virgin, Altar, Church and Cemetery. Each finely produced illumination has a brief note by the scholarly hand of Frere. The manuscript probably comes from Western Germany, whereas those used in the first part of the work, Collection III, Vol. 1, were English manuscripts.

V DEARMER, PERCY. Dat Boexken van der Missen: 'The Booklet of the Mass' by Brother Gherit van der Goude, 1507. The thirty-four plates described, and the explanatory text of the Flemish original translated, with illustrative excerpts from contemporary missals and tracts. pp. xvi, 156, 35 ill., Longmans, Green; 1903.

Thirty-four 16th century woodcuts, illustrating the celebration of the Mass, are here reproduced in black and white. They are taken from the only complete edition of *Dat Boexken van der Missen*, which was printed in Antwerp in 1507. The Booklet consists of three short books. The first and third are devotional works typical of the period, while the second contains the plates here reproduced. The work, used as the basis of Dearmer's, is divided into thirty-three 'articles' being illustrated by sixty-seven plates, providing a detailed description of the Mass. The pictures offer a valuable visible commentary on the ceremonial used at a High Mass of the period.

VI EELES, F. C. Ed., From transcripts by BROWN, J. E. The Edwardian Inventories for Bedfordshire. pp. xxii, 43, Longmans, Green; 1905.

During its long history the Alcuin Club has published a number of valuable Inventories making available, to liturgists and historians alike, a most useful series of printed prime source material. English Inventories provide a collection of historic documents without parallel in any other country. Produced in the 16th century, as a preparation for the wholesale seizure of ecclesiastical property, they give an unrivalled insight into the church furniture and ornaments of that period. On March 3rd, 1551 the Privy Council ordered 'that for as much as the Kinges Majestie had neede presently of a masse of mooney, therfore Commissions shulde be addressed into all shires of Englande to take into the Kinges hands suche churche plate as remaigneth, to be emploied unto his highnes use'. On January 16th, 1553 a new commission was issued directing the actual seizure of all the valuables, only the barest necessities being left for the use of each church.

All the plate so seized was sent to the Jewel House in the Tower of London and melted down, the vestments and any inferior metal work were sold locally. This systematic collection of church property, by Royal Injunction, was most thoroughly carried out as a result of the carefully prepared Inventories.

Only 14 of the 125 Edwardian Inventories, taken in Bedfordshire in 1552, have come down to us. These are reproduced in this work, along with Marian documents relating to Bedfordshire Church Goods. A list of names of persons is also included.

VII LOMAS, S. C. Ed., From transcripts by CRAIB, T. The Edwardian Inventories for Huntingdonshire. pp. xxx, 57, Longmans, Green; 1906.

When these Inventories were taken, in the 6th year of King Edward VI (1552), there were about ninety parishes in the county of Huntingdon. The Inventories of thirty-six of these parishes are still extant, plus useless fragments of three others. These Inventories tell of a wide range of ecclesiastical property, copes, vestment sets, albes and ammesses, rochettes and tunacles, altar clothes and banner clothes, towelles and surplesses, crosses and candellstickes, holliewater stoppes and sillver senseres, challices and pyxes, steople and sauntus belles. These Inventories from a good third of the parishes provide a most interesting insight into the life and worship of the church in a period of flux. There is also a section on Church Goods sold or stolen in the county of Huntingdon and a collection of miscellaneous documents.

VIII EELES, F. C. Ed., Pontifical Services. Illustrated from woodcuts of the XVIth Century with descriptive notes. Volume III, pp. 145, 72 ill., Longmans, Green; 1907.

This volume continues the study of Pontifical Services begun by Frere in Collections III and IV. Seventy-two illustrated pages give some 143 figures, reproducing woodcuts from two Roman Pontificals printed in Venice in 1520 and 1572. The range of subjects is much wider than the previous volumes and includes such items as Confirmation, delivery of Candle to Acolytes, the Litany, Coronation of the Pope, Veiling of Abbess and the Blessing of a new Knight, to name but a few. Pithy notes are given to each illustration.

IX EELES, F. C. Ed., From transcripts by BROWN, J. E. The Edwardian Inventories for Buckinghamshire. pp. lii, 157, Longmans, Green; 1908.

The suppression of the monasteries, by Henry VIII, extended to colleges, chantries and free chapels. Early in the reign of Edward VI, this work of sacrilege and confiscation reached out even to the parish churches. Early in 1549 a commission for making Inventories was issued to Sheriffs and Justices of the Peace. Due to these Inventories the seizure of church plate and ornaments was greatly assisted.

Buckinghamshire has preserved some 170 Inventories; twenty-eight of these, taken in 1553, relate to goods left by the Commissioners for use in the churches in the hundred of Buckingham, after the rest had been taken to raise money for the king. Of the 142 remaining Inventories covering 126 parishes, some are duplicates and others fragmentary, leaving, for practical purposes some 123 Inventories. A most informative Introduction, 5 appendixes and an index of names, add to the value of this work.

X DEARMER, PERCY. Fifty Pictures of Gothic Altars. pp. 211, 50 ill., Longmans, Green; 1910.

A supplement to Collection I, which consisted exclusively of pictures of English altars, this work brings together a series of fifty medieval altars, including Continental sources. It was produced 'for the benefit of architects and of others concerned in the arrangement and decoration of churches.' By means of these reproductions and the annotations attached to each one, the subject of the altar and its use in Western Europe, during the Gothic period, is carefully covered. The pictures are full of interest and give a clear idea of the altar and its architectural setting during the period. They also illustrate other features, lecterns, vestments of ministers, plate and altar furnishings etc. The miniatures are not confined to the use of the altar for the Mass but cover a number of subjects e.g. division of the first fruits, Martyrdoms, Funerals, and Visions.

XI WARREN, FREDERICK. E. The Sarum Missal in English: pp. Volume I, xv, 425; Volume II, 640, Mowbray; 1913.

For this English translation of the Sarum Missal, Warren used the folio printed edition of 1526, copies of which are lodged in the Bodleian Library, Oxford, and the University Library, Cambridge. The translation thus makes available to the English reader a text not easily accessible.

Part I covers the Kalendar, Blessing of Salt and Water, Asperges, Blessing of Bread on Sundays, Prayers before Mass, Ordinary of the Mass, Canon of the Mass, Thanksgiving after Mass, Prayers in Prostration, Prayers after Mass, Mass in Remembrance of the Feasts of the B.V.M., Propers of Seasons, Anniversary of Dedication of a Church, Consecration of a Church, Reconciliation of a Church. Part 2 contains Common of Saints, Votive Masses, Common Memories, Order of Matrimony, Mass in honour of the B.V.M., Order of Service for Pilgrims, Office for the Dead, Mass to turn away Pestilence, Passion of Pope John XXII, Mass of St Sebastian in time of Pestilence, Commemorative Masses of SS. Erasmus, Roch, Christopher, Anthony, Raphael, Gabriel, Mass of the Compassion of the B.V.M.,

Mass of St Barbara, Prayers of the Passion of our Lord, Of the Kyrie Eleison, Proper of Saints.

In addition to the useful Introduction in Part 1, Part 2 contains a scriptural index, index of proper names, and a general index and glossary.

XII RILEY, ATHELSTAN. Ed., Pontifical Services: Illustrated from woodcuts of the XVIth Century. Volume IV, pp. viii, 149, 73 ill., Longmans, Green; 1908.

This volume continues the work begun in Collection VIII, Vol. III, illustrating the services of the Roman Pontifical about the time of the Reformation, by reproducing woodcuts from the Venice editions of 1520 and 1572, used in Vol. III, each woodcut being accompanied by descriptive notes. A wide range of subjects are included e.g., forty-one reproductions on the consecration of a church, the consecration of a churchyard, blessing of vestments, a bell, armour and a sword, Holy Week ceremonies, and various other services. To the observant and well-trained eye the 134 reproductions on the seventy-three illustrated pages offer a mine of information on ecclesiastical life, property, and services during the 16th century.

XIII ATCHLEY, E. G. CUTHBERT F. A History of the use of Incense in Divine Worship. pp. xxix, 404, 50 ill., Longmans, Green; 1909.

With the largest pagination of any Alcuin publication, this is a magisterial historic investigation of a complex and fascinating subject. A descriptive list of the 50 pages of illustrations is followed by Part 1, on the Non-Christian Use of Incense. The writer contends that the non-Christian origin of the use of incense is no argument against its use in the Catholic

Church. Included in this section is a survey on its use in Oriental religions and in pagan Greece and Rome, and some reflections as to the theory of its use. The Christian use of incense from the earliest days, in both East and Western Christendom, is carefully documented. The purpose, occasions and ceremonies attached to the use of incense, supported by a mass of footnotes, are clearly given in a most readable form. The use of incense in England during the reigns of Edward VI and Elizabeth is covered in the last chapter of Part 2. An appendix gives rules for censing from various English rites. A very short index is included.

XIV FRERE, WALTER HOWARD. Visitation Articles and Injunctions of the Period of the Reformation, Volume I, Historical Introduction and Index. pp. xvi, 385, Longmans, Green; 1910.

This is the first of three volumes, produced out of Frere's encyclopedic storehouse of knowledge on ecclesiastical documents. He gives the purpose of these volumes as: (i) to give a more complete series than has been hitherto accessible; (ii) by cross references, footnotes, and an elaborate index to elucidate them in relation to one another and to current events; and (iii) to place the whole series in its setting by the introduction tracing the origin and development of the practice of Visitation and its special relation to the Reformation changes. These Articles give a vivid picture of the changes in the religious life of 16th-century England. From them the historian can trace the year by year, sometime even month by month, gradual alterations in the ecclesiastical life of this country. While all English Episcopal registries and numerous archives were searched in preparation for this work, nevertheless, Frere admitted that he had not exhausted the subject.

This volume contains a long Introduction on the subject of Visitations. Seven appendixes and a list of principal authorities are followed by the general index to the documents in Volumes II and III. This 170 page index covers a limitless number of subjects and offers a valuable guide to church historians of the period.

XV FRERE, WALTER HOWARD and KENNEDY, WILLIAM McCLURE. Visitation Articles and Injunctions of the Period of the Reformation, Volume II, 1536-1558. pp. viii, 426, Longmans, Green; 1910.

Following the historical introduction to the subject of Visitation in Volume I, this second volume ranges from the Royal Visitation of 1536 to the close of Mary's reign. The book contains not only Royal Injunctions but also Injunctions by Latimer, Lee, Fox, Cranmer, Bonner, Ridley, Hooper, and Poole, to name but a few.

XVI FRERE, WALTER HOWARD Ed., Visitation Articles and Injunctions of the Period of Reformation, Volume III, 1559-1575. pp. viii, 386, Longmans, Green; 1910.

This third· volume on the Articles and Injunctions of the Reformation Period is concerned with the primacy of Matthew Parker, 1559-1575. Beginning with the Royal Articles of Queen Elizabeth in 1559, there are also Royal Injunctions for a number of Cathedrals and Cambridge University. Articles and Injunctions by Parker, Jewel, Grindal, Horne, and others are also included.

With this volume a most useful and reliable source of historic documents is completed.

XVII EELES, F. C. Traditional Ceremonial and Customs connected with the Scottish Liturgy. pp. xi, 175, Longmans, Green; 1910.

Perhaps the most unusual feature of this work is the fact that it is based upon oral traditions, and not upon written or printed liturgical sources. Assisted by many friends, the author collected together a number of traditional ceremonial customs connected with the rendering of the Scottish Liturgy and other services of the Church. An impartial presentation of the material is made with no attempt at selection, thus good and bad are included together. The work is intended as a book for liturgical students, and not as a directory for church use. Amongst the subjects covered are Church Furniture and Clerical Dress, Preparation of the Eucharistic Elements, The Liturgy, Reservation of the Eucharist, Mattins and Evensong and the Occasional Services.

XVIII COBB, CYRIL S. The Rationale of Ceremonial 1540-1543: with notes and appendices and an essay on the Regulation of Ceremonial during the reign of King Henry VIII, with four facsimiles of handwriting. pp. lxxv, 80, 4 ill., Longmans, Green; 1910.

In this work the difference in the immediate external pretexts for the Reformation on the Continent and in England, is examined along the lines of the difference of Standpoint, Method, the test applied and the external circumstances. How this difference affected the treatment of ceremonial in England and on the Continent is considered. In England the old system was much favoured and so attempts were made to modify this system by means of authoritative declarations. After this brief introductory survey of the subject, *The Book concerning Ceremonies to be used in the Church of England*

1540-1543 is reproduced from the Lambeth Manuscript 1107. Four appendixes provide further useful documentation on the subject. A good index is also included.

XIX SKILBECK, CLEMENT O. and DEARMER, PERCY. Illustrations of the Liturgy: Being thirteen drawings of the celebration of the Holy Communion in a Parish Church. pp. 85, 15 ill., Mowbray; 1912.

The need of order, ceremonial direction, and embellishment, firmly based on the Prayer Book, in place of disorder and the use of Roman ceremonial, was the chief cause of this publication.

Twelve drawings are used to illustrate the Sunday Eucharist with full ceremonial and the full complement of ministers, as used in many parts of the Anglican Communion at the time of publication. What is illustrated and commented upon is the 'English Use' of the Prayer Book, as used in the greater part of the Anglican Communion. Three appendixes are included (i) Readers of the Gospel and Epistle; (ii) a plan showing a convenient arrangement of the east end of a town church; (iii) Notes on Mattins, Litany, and the Communion.

XX CRESSWELL, BEATRIX F. The Edwardian Inventories for the City and County of Exeter; Transcribed from the original documents in the Guildhall, Exeter. pp. xvi, 90, Mowbray; 1916.

Inventories were normally held at the Public Record Office. In Exeter, however, only nine were thus lodged, the rest being preserved in the Exeter Guildhall. The Exeter Collection contains not only the Interrogatories and the parchment Inventories signed by the bishop and commissioners, but rough copies of the Inventories on paper signed by the

Churchwardens, and the actual lists of church goods that were handed in from each parish. Because of their special and somewhat unusual nature these hand-written lists, produced by the Churchwardens, are of great interest. There seems to have been an attempt to include every item of possible value. Documents from Exeter Cathedral and twenty-one parishes are included in this volume and a list relating to each church is given at the beginning of each parish; because of repetitions, not all are printed. A name-index is included.

XXI FREESTONE, W. H. The Sacrament Reserved: A survey of the practice of reserving the Eucharist, with special reference to the communion of the sick, during the first twelve centuries. pp. viii, 281, Mowbray; 1917.

Anticipating the charge of inadequacy, Freestone acknowledges certain limitations in this work: (i) in not going beyond the Fourth Lateran Council, 1215; (ii) in the section on the place of reservation; (iii) in the history of reservation in the East. He then goes on to give a masterly survey of his subject, within the limits he has set. Having examined the terms Ephodion and Viaticum he looks at 'Official' distribution from the Public Celebration of the Liturgy, beginning in the time of Justin. Private reservation by the Laity, Religious and the Clergy, and the use of the reserved Eucharist at Ordination, followed by a section on the: Peculiar uses of the reserved Eucharist; Eulogiae, Fermentum, Sancta, Communion of the Presanctified, Consumption of the Remains and Administration to the dead, are all covered in Part I. The remainder of the work deals with 'Official reservation for the Communion of the Sick'. Seventy pages are given to a historic survey of 'Official Reservation'.

A number of connected issues are then studied, e.g.,

renewal of the reserved sacrament, place and vessels, the minister of the reserved sacrament, clinical communion and some Eastern Customs. An appendix gives brief details of the beginnings of the extra-liturgical cultus of the Eucharist. An 11-page, double-columned index and a list of principal authorities add to the value of this work.

XXII CLAYTON, H. J. The Ornaments of the Ministers as shown on English Monumental Brasses. pp. 190, 83 ill., Mowbray; 1919.

Monumental brasses are shown, by Clayton to be of considerable value as a guide to the dress of ecclesiastics from the 13th to the 17th century. He contends that they provide an abundance of evidence for the interpretation of the Ornaments Rubric in the BCP, so far as the ornaments of the minister which were used in the second half of the reign of Edward VI are concerned. In this work he limits himself to those brasses which illustrate his theory. Each illustration is accompanied by notes on the various items worn. Three indexes on persons, places, and dates are included.

XXIII GRAHAM, ROSE Ed., From transcripts by CRAIB, T. The Chantry Certificates for Oxfordshire and the Edwardian Inventories of Church Goods for Oxfordshire. pp. xxxi, 147, Mowbray; 1920.

Chantry Certificates and the Inventories of Church Goods describe endowments and possessions of which the parish churches were almost entirely deprived during the reign of Edward VI. Because of their universities, Oxford and Cambridge were not included in the ordinary county commission, and two special bodies of commissioners were appointed by the King. The special nature of Oxford, its

Inventories and the Chantry Act and related issues, are admirably dealt with in the Introduction to this work. Not all the available material is included, but it does contain a wide range of historic documentation on Chantry Certificates of the city of Oxford, 1547, and for Oxfordshire, 1548, plus a large number of Edwardian Inventories for Oxfordshire. An appendix on the foundation dates of Chantries and Guilds, a brief glossary and a name index are also included.

XXIV KINGSFORD, H. S. Illustrations of the Occasional Offices of the Church in the Middle Ages from Contemporary Sources. pp. iv, 89, 46 ill., Mowbray; 1921.

This is a book of pictures, with brief notes, illustrating the various rites and ceremonies in which a layman had his part in the Middle Ages. These interesting pictures, not always to be interpreted too literally, provide a glimpse of the religious life of the medieval layman from his birth to his death. For the sake of completeness, representations of the Communion, while not an Occasional Office, are included. Thus there is the following sequence: baptism, confirmation, penance, communion, marriage, death, unction and burial.

XXV KENNEDY, W. P. M. Elizabethan Episcopal Administration: An Essay in Sociology and Politics. Volume I, pp. ccxlix, Mowbray; 1924.

Three volumes, of which this is the first, on Elizabethan Episcopal Administration, continue the earlier joint work by Frere and Kennedy on the *Visitation Articles and Injunctions of the Period of the Reformation*, Alcuin Collections XIV, XV and XVI. After six volumes no claim is made to have exhausted the subject. Visitation Articles and Injunctions from the death of Parker 1575 to the close of Elizabeth's reign are given in Volumes II, and III, which are seen as the completion of the previous joint work.

Volume I contains Kennedy's Essay, based on the documents of 1558-1603, which provides a valuable chapter on Elizabethan history, pursued along political and sociological lines. Here a new sovereignty is seen in action with its weapons of divine right and of *cujus regio ejus religio*, a chapter in political absolutism. The sociological aspect of this work illustrates the daily life of the people of the period. A number of useful statistical tables are included.

Eight chapters guide the reader through a labyrinth of material on the permanent forces at work in administration, the Parish Church, Clergy, Laity, Parish Officials, Puritan and Recusant and the Tudor Political Theory. An appendix, giving authorities and sources, and a good index are also provided.

XXVI KENNEDY, W. P. M. Elizabethan Episcopal Administration: Visitation Articles and Injunctions, 1575-1582. Volume II, pp. 135, Mowbray; 1924.

Twenty-five documents are reproduced in this volume along with foot and marginal notes. Beginning with Bishop Blethyn's Constitutions for Llandaff Cathedral in 1576, there are Articles and Injunctions, covering the eight years of 1575-1582, for such places as the Cathedrals of Canterbury, Bangor, Gloucester, Rochester, Peterborough, Worcester, and York, for the Dioceses of Lincoln, London, Chichester, Worcester, Durham, and Chester, and these by the hands of such men as Grindal, Pier, Whitgift, Sandys, and Aylmer, to name only some.

XXVII KENNEDY, W. P. M. Elizabethan Episcopal Administration: Visitation Articles and Injunctions, 1583-1603. Volume III, pp. 214, Mowbray; 1924.

With this volume, Kennedy's three-volume work, primarily intended as a documentary source for historians, is concluded. Forty-two Articles and Injunctions, by the hands of Archbishop Whitgift, fifteen Bishops and three Archdeacons, addressed to some fifteen Dioceses, seven Cathedrals, three Archdeaconries, one Deanery and to the Provinces of Canterbury and York, are carefully reproduced and indexed.

XXVIII FRERE, WALTER HOWARD. Studies in Early Roman Liturgy, I. The Kalendar. pp. 159, OUP; 1930.

Collections XXVIII, XXX, and XXXII, compose a trilogy of studies in the Early Roman Liturgy by the erudite hand of Frere. Volume I studies the Kalendar of the Roman Church which lies at the roots of the development of the Kalendar in almost all the historic churches of the West. Part 1 critically examines the available evidence about the Kalendar and challenges some generally accepted views, especially about Sacramentaries. From this examination of a considerable amount of material some idea is given of the stages in the growth of the Roman Kalendar. Eleven chapters cover the Martyrology, Tituli, Deaconries, Stations, Suburban Cemeteries and Shrines, Leonine, Gelasian, Gregorian and Mixed Sacramentaries, Lectionaries and Choir-books. Part 2 examines the various entries in the Kalendar, their liturgical order, and the antiquity of their claim to a place there. Five indexes covering authorities, abbreviations, service books, places, and saints and their churches, conclude this volume.

XXIX TYRER, JOHN WALTON. Historical Survey of Holy Week: its Services and Ceremonial. pp. xix, 180, OUP; 1932.

The first three chapters of this work provide a history of Holy Week, from the first century to the end of the seventh, covering the Church of both East and West. Chapter four begins the second section of the book, which is limited to the Church of the West and more particularly to the Roman and Gallican rites. Three English Uses are given special mention, the medieval Uses of Sarum, York, and Canterbury. This section gives an admirable detailed historical sketch of the various Western Holy Week services. Two lists giving service-books and principal authorities precede the body of the work, and give some indication as to the vast number of sources used and the depth of the scholarship behind this Collection. There is also a six-page double-column index.

XXX FRERE, WALTER HOWARD. Studies in the Early Roman Liturgy, II. The Roman Gospel-Lectionary. pp. vi, 247, OUP; 1934.

Forty years of gradual collecting and comparing of capitularies, i.e., schemes of the Mass-lessons, to be found in Gospel-books, lay behind this second volume of studies in Early Roman Liturgy. The complexity of the subject and the mass of available documentation make this a most bewildering and yet most interesting field of research. Frere limits his inquiry to the Roman rite and covers only four centuries, from A.D. 700 onwards. From his study of the Gospel-books he traces a fairly clear line of historical development, although details remain somewhat obscure. He begins with the 'Earlier Series' received by Pippin in the mid 8th century, moving on to the 'Standard Series' (in two forms), representing the models promulgated by Charlemagne at the end of the 8th century. These are compared, and common features noted. Further types and developments are examined, leading on to a study of the disintegration of the 'Standard Series' and the Gelasian influence. Six indexes are included covering sources, persons, bibliography, places, abbreviations, liturgical days and general index. This is a scholarly work intended for the specialist.

XXXI ATCHLEY, E. G. CUTHBERT F. On the Epiclesis of the Eucharistic Liturgy and in the Consecration of the Font. pp. vi, 210, OUP; 1935.

This systematic study of the Fathers and early Liturgies bears witness to the existence of a prayer for the consecration of the Eucharist and the blessing of the baptismal water, which shares with the materials of the Eucharistic Offering the same quality of being inanimate. In both cases the usual prayer contains a petition that the Holy Spirit may hallow them. This petition came to be called an epiclesis or invocation; used in a technical sense, both words have exactly the same meaning. While the effect of the divine intervention in these two cases is quite different, in both cases the Holy Spirit is asked to hallow inanimate matter and not merely the souls of believers. After an introductory study, as to the meaning of epiclesis, Atchley gives forty-five compact chapters of documentation, beginning with the New Testament and followed by Ignatius, Justin, and Irenaeus. He moves on to examine evidence from Africa, Rome, Egypt, Syria, Jerusalem, Italy, Armenia, ending with the English divines of the 16th and 17th centuries. A brief conclusion summing up the results of the examination is followed by a good index.

XXXII FRERE, WALTER HOWARD. Studies in the Early Roman Liturgy, III. The Roman Epistle-Lectionary. pp. vi, 115, OUP; 1935.

Frere's work on the early Roman Lectionaries of the Mass began with Collection XXX, where he examined the Gospel-Capitularies, and for which study he had gathered an abundance of material. Work on the Lectionaries of Epistles is made difficult by the scantiness of available material, which leads to inevitable gaps. The two Capitularies, in general, share the same method, and passages are allotted as being proper to particular days. He shows how four things are taken into account: (i) the great feasts and fasts of the Christian year, with the seasons belonging to them; (ii) the saints to be commemorated; (iii) special occasions, especially those connected with Baptism, Ordinations and Embertides; (iv) the localities in which the services were to be held. Nine somewhat brief passages cover the following subjects: the Sources, A Comparison of Earlier and Standard Series, Alcuin's Lectionary, Development and Manuscripts, the 'Comes', the Sanctorale of the 'Comes', Gospels of the 'Comes' manuscripts, Theotinchus, and Composite Lessons. Five indexes cover sources; persons, subjects, and bibliography; places; abbreviations; and liturgical days. There is also a Schedule of Liturgical Epistles and Lessons. Once again, this is a specialist work.

XXXIII PERKINS, JOCELYN. Westminster Abbey, its Worship and Ornaments, Vol. I. pp. xxi, 194, 31 ill., OUP; 1938.

Many books have been published on Westminster Abbey and, as it is an epitome of English history, this is to be expected. Because of its many facets, such a vast subject can warrant a number of major works, and the last word on the subject has not yet been said. This volume is a study in depth of the worship of the Abbey; worship being used in a very broad sense, going beyond ceremonial and ritual and including the ornaments or instruments of worship. A ten-page introductory chapter is followed by Part II, which has fifteen chapters dealing with the High Altar and Presbytery. Part III, confined to the Choir, has eight chapters.

XXXIV PERKINS, JOCELYN. Westminster Abbey, its Worship and Ornaments, Vol. II. pp. xvi, 215, 35 ill., OUP; 1940.

As in Volume I, the beautifully produced plates, are not mere embellishments, having been carefully chosen out of literally thousands of possible illustrations; they play an important part in the work, and are reproduced upon a definite plan. Each of the three volumes contain notes on the illustrations used. This volume covers the Rood-Screen, the Pulpitum, the Altars of the Nave, the Chapel of St Edward the Confessor, the Chantry Chapel of Henry V, and the Chapel of King Henry VII. Historic material is presented in this, and indeed in all three volumes, in an interesting and readable fashion.

XXXV ARNOLD, J. H. and WYATT, E. G. P. Walter Howard Frere, A collection of his Papers on Liturgical and Historical subjects. pp. xv, 232, 2 ill., OUP; 1940.

The Alcuin Club owes a great deal to Walter Howard Frere, a member of the Committee from the inception of the Club and for many years its President. One of the greatest liturgical scholars in the history of the Church of England, he produced more Alcuin publications than any other author.

This volume and Collection XXXIX were published as a mark of the Club's respect for this outstanding liturgical scholar. A number of essays and papers written by Frere on various subjects are here reproduced in a permanent form. The subjects covered are too many to list, but include the Connexion between English and Norman Rites, Lollardy and the Reformation, the Use of Exeter, Gloria in Excelsis, the Christian Altar, Reservation in Elizabethan Days, Funerals, and Early Franciscan influence on Religious Services, to name but a few. A bibliography of Frere's many publications is also included.

XXXVI DUNCAN-JONES, A. S. The Chichester Customary: The rites of the Church as observed throughout the year in Chichester Cathedral. pp. xxii, 92, 13 ill., SPCK; 1948.
The Customary of Chichester Cathedral is so called because it embodies the actual customs in use in the conduct of the services in the cathedral church. Whilst this work was originally compiled for practical and domestic reasons, a wider interest led to its publication. Ceremonial directions given in the work are based upon the rites contained in *The Book of Common Prayer with the Additions and Deviations proposed in 1928*. Amongst the subjects covered are the Daily Offices, Holy Communion, Burial of the Dead, Ordination, Blessing of Crib, Carol Service, Lent Use, Lights, and Liturgical Colours. Five Forms and Offices are given and nine notes covering such things as Incense, the Offertory, the Elevation, Standing, Kneeling, Sitting, and Plough Sunday. Amongst the illustrations are plates and a number of ceremonial diagrams.

XXXVII RATCLIFF, EDWARD C. The Booke of Common Prayer of the Churche of England, its making and revisions 1549-1661 set forth in eighty illustrations with introductory notes. pp. 120, 80 ill., SPCK; 1949.

Produced with the non-specialist in mind, this work was published to mark the 400th anniversary of the BCP. Unlike most books written about the BCP, this little work appeals primarily to the eye, and not the mind. Eighty illustrations reproduce pages from pre-Reformation service books and from successive editions of the English Prayer Book. From these clear reproductions the reader is given some idea as to the nature and appearance of the service books of our pre-Reformation 'fathers-in-the-faith'. Each plate has a brief commentary and there is a short, non-technical, introduction to the Prayer Book. Overall, we have a simple and yet enchanting volume.

XXXVIII PERKINS, JOCELYN. Westminster Abbey, its Worship and Ornaments, Vol. III. pp. xii, 239, 17 ill., OUP; 1952.

With this volume Perkins completes his three-volume work on the 'Worship' of England's foremost Abbey. A most fascinating range of subjects is covered. The eleven eastern chapels are dealt with in the first section. The second section, 'The Furniture', covers the pulpits, font, litany, stools, lecterns, gates, and floors. A section on 'The Ornaments' deals with the 16th- and 17th-century plate, verges and maces, and the ancient fabrics. Worship and Order during the period 1560-1950 takes up the last and main part of the work. There are eight appendixes which include four Inventories compiled between 1520 and 1750. A long index, which covers all three volumes, completes this volume, and at the same time what must be regarded as a standard work for students of things Westmonasterian.

XXXIX JASPER, RONALD C. D. Ed. Walter Howard Frere: His Correspondence on Liturgical Revision and Construction. pp. xiii, 317, 1 ill., SPCK; 1954.

A bundle of letters by Frere which he thought might be of value for publication at some future date are here reproduced. Like all Frere's written work, this collection of liturgical correspondence discloses the breadth and depth of his liturgical scholarship and, at the same time, shows how he was able to penetrate to the root of the issues before him. Written originally without any thought of publication, these letters reveal much of the man himself, his sincerity, saintliness, objectivity, and deep respect for the other man's point of view.

The documents are reproduced as written, and simply set in their context and allowed to speak for themselves. In this way they act as a kind of commentary on the liturgical developments within the Anglican Communion during Frere's day. Part 1, Liturgical Revision in England, covers: the Early Days, Advisory Committee on Liturgical Questions, Rearrangement of the Canon, Initial work in the Church Assembly, The House of Bishops, the Canon and Reservation Final Stages, and Opposition; Part 2, Liturgical Revision in other parts of the Anglican Communion, covers: The Lambeth Conference 1920, Japan, South Africa, Northern Rhodesia, Hebrew Christians, South India, and Ceylon. There are two appendixes and a useful index.

45

XL GRISBROOKE, W. JARDINE. Anglican Liturgies of the Seventeenth and Eighteenth Centuries. pp. xvi, 390, SPCK; 1958.

The rites of the Church of England emerged from the English Reformation of the 16th century, and both their liturgical structure and underlying doctrine bear the impression of one man – Thomas Crammer. Whilst many have been satisfied with the services finally formulated in the 1662 BCP, others have criticised them and worked for their revision. A widespread dissatisfaction, due to the feeling that these services no longer suffice to serve the needs of the worshipping community today, has been a recurring theme of this century.

In this volume Grisbrooke examines some attempts made to revise the rite of Holy Communion during the 17th and 18th centuries. In all, eleven rites are reproduced, along with an introductory commentary to each. They are not of equal value or interest, but together they offer a most useful collection of rites. Beginning with the Scottish Liturgy of 1637, Grisbrooke then reproduces the Liturgy of Jeremy Taylor, the Liturgies of Edward Stephens, William Whiston and John Henley, the Nonjurors' Liturgies of 1718 and 1734, the Liturgy of Thomas Rattray, and the Scottish Liturgy of 1764.

There is an appendix containing, in the hand of William Sancroft, amendments proposed during the revision of the Holy Communion in 1661. Bibliographical notes and a good index complete the work.

XLI DENDY, D. R. The Use of Lights in Christian Worship. pp. xiii, 197, SPCK; 1959.

The early Fathers were clearly hostile to the symbolic use of lights in worship, and it is not until the 4th century that the ceremonial use of lights in Christian worship became firmly established. Once the use was established, there was a rapid increase in the practice which found expression in many of the Church's rites. Eleven chapters describe the beginnings and developments of each custom. With some exceptions in English and Gallican uses, the practices are traced to the time of the Reformation. Reference to the use of the Eastern Church is confined to the earlier centuries. Lights as Ornaments around and upon the Altar take up the first three chapters. The remaining chapters cover the Use of lights in the Mass, Cult of the Departed, Candles at Funerals, Cult of the Saints, Lights in Baptism, Ceremonies of Holy Week, Post-Reformation Usage in England and Other Customs-Candlemas, Benediction, and the Dedication of Churches. An excellent bibliography and short index complete this most readable work.

XLII WHITAKER, E. C. Documents of the Baptismal Liturgy. pp. viii, 220, SPCK; 1960.

Liturgical scholars and students, especially those interested in Christian Initiation, are deeply indebted to Whitaker for providing this most useful collection of not easily obtainable documents. Some forty English translations are brought together and presented in a clear and orderly fashion. Chapter one contains seven documents belonging to the Ante-Nicene Church, while the remaining documents are grouped together in geographical areas covering some ten chapters: Syria, Armenia, Byzantine, Egypt, Africa, Spain, Milan, Rome, Gallican, and Hybrid documents. A final chapter contains a number of canons produced by local Councils in the West. In 1970 this work was revised and an Introductory Essay, 'The Sacrament of Christian Initiation', and the Sarum Rite, in English, were added.

XLIII WIGAN, BERNARD. Ed. The Liturgy in English. pp. xvi, 250, OUP; 1962.

Tract XXII of the Alcuin Club offered the English reader a useful collection of Anglican Liturgies edited by J. H. Arnold. This present volume both replaces and extends the scope of the earlier publication. Part 1 contains the following rites: the English Liturgies of 1549, 1662, the Scottish Liturgy, the American Liturgy, the Proposed English Revision (1928), the South African, Ceylon, Bombay, Indian (1960), Japanese and Canadian (1959), Liturgies, also the Liturgies of the Dioceses of Nyasaland and Northern Rhodesia, the Swahili Mass, the Liturgies of the Church in Korea and the Church of the Province of the West Indies. Part 2 contains four non-Anglican liturgies: The Directory, the Book of Common Order, A Congregationalist Liturgy, and the Liturgy of the Church of South India. There are five appendixes which cover Proper Prefaces, Offertory Sentences, Post Communion Collects, Introits and Graduals, and Supplementary Consecration. While it is admitted that other rites could have been included, nevertheless this is a wide ranging collection of Eucharistic rites, each with a brief introduction, presented and preserved in a most useful and handy form.

XLIV WILLIS, G. G. St Augustine's Lectionary. pp. ix, 115, SPCK; 1962.

There is little information concerning lectionary schemes before the seventh century and therefore Dr Willis' research in this field has proved most valuable. With meticulous care he has examined the sermons of St Augustine and from these has been able to give some idea as to the lectionary in use in Africa, during the 4th-5th centuries. Before examining the works of St Augustine he looks at the Lectionary System before St Augustine and the Lectionary of St Ambrose. In Part two, which takes up nearly half of the book, he deals with St Augustine's Lectionary. Part three 'Some Later Lectionaries and their contacts with St Augustine's Lectionary' has chapters on Syriac, Mozarabic, Gallican, Ambrosian and North Italian, Roman, Neapolitan, and Anglo-Saxon Lectionaries. An appendix to this section gives, in tabular form, the Lectionary schemes of St Peter Chrysologus, St Maximus of Turin, and St Leo the Great. A bibliography of sources, and indexes on scripture quotations, days and seasons, and proper names complete the work.

XLV DUGMORE, C. W. The Influence of the Synagogue upon the Divine Office. pp. viii, 151, Faith Press; 1964.

This work was first published in 1944. Because of the interest in the subject, and at the same time the lack of further studies in this field, the Alcuin Club suggested that they should reprint the work as their 1964 Collection.

There is no doubt that Judaism, and especially the Synagogue, had a tremendous influence upon the development of early Christian worship. The content of the services and the development of the monastic Hours both bear the mark of this influence.

Supported by a wide range of documentation, the author guides his reader, in the course of eight brief chapters, through an important and fascinating subject. He deals with the Early Christian Community, the Services of the Synagogue, the Christian Week, Growth of the Canonical Hours, The Pro-Anaphora – its early outline and development in the 4th and 5th centuries, and the Jewish contribution. A glossary, bibliography, and indexes on Biblical References, Patristic Literature, Rabbinic References, and Subjects and

49

Names, enhance the value of the work and give the interested reader source-material to enable further research.

XLVI WILLIS, G. G. Essays in Early Roman Liturgy. pp. viii, 147, SPCK; 1964.

Six essays on subjects concerning the Roman rite in the early Middle Ages, with the addition of a short but excellent bibliography, and three indexes, make up this brief but scholarly work. The essays investigate the following subjects: The Solemn Prayers of Good Friday, Ember Days, What is *Mediana* Week?, The Offertory Prayers and the Canon of the Roman Mass, *Cursus* in the Roman Canon, The Connection of the Prayers of the Roman Canon.

XLVII FISHER, J. D. C. Christian Initiation – Baptism in the Medieval West: A study in the disintegration of the Primitive rite of initiation. pp. xiii, 203, SPCK; 1965.

While much has been written about baptism in the New Testament, the wider field of Christian Initiation, including its liturgical aspects and doctrine, and its history and development, have been sadly neglected. Fisher's scholarly and well-documented work thus makes a much-needed contribution to this subject. Certain limits are set on the work in that it is confined to the Medieval period and to the West. The disintegration of the established rite of the 7th century is traced, showing that the division into three separate parts, and seemingly independent rites of baptism, confirmation and first communion, was brought about by non-theological factors.

Beginning with Christian Initiation in Rome from John the Deacon and the Gelasian Sacramentary of the 12th century, he goes on to consider the subject in Milan and Northern Italy from Ambrose to the *Ordo of Beroldus*. Next, he looks at the situation in Gaul and Germany from the 7th to the 12th century, and in the British Isles from Augustine of Canterbury to the 12th century.

The final section of this geographical survey deals with Spain from Isidore of Seville to the Mozarabic *Liber Ordinum*. The Separation of Communion from Initiation, the Shortening of the interval between Birth and Baptism, and the Lengthening of the interval between Baptism and Confirmation, make up the last three chapters. Six appendixes, a good bibliography, and indexes of subjects and proper names complete a work which is essential reading for any who wish to understand the initiatory rites of the BCP.

XLVIII MITCHELL, LEONEL, L. Baptismal Anointing. pp. xvii, 199, SPCK; 1966.

Within the Anglican Communion, the question as to the moment and means by which the Holy Spirit is conferred in the Initiatory process, is still a matter of much debate. Confining himself to one aspect of the initiatory rite, the anointing with oil which accompanies baptism in all Christian liturgies from at least the 3rd to the 15th centuries, Dr Mitchell makes a most worthwhile contribution to the ongoing debate. Whilst the work is largely liturgical and historical, the author does not refrain from making 'interpretative theological comments.' Dividing it into five parts, he examines evidence from *The Apostolic Tradition*, Origins of Baptismal Anointing, Ancient Syrian Rites, Eastern Rites, and the Western Rites. Two appendixes cover the Anglican Use of Baptismal Oil and the Seal of the Spirit. There is a select bibliography and subject- and name-indexes.

51

XLIX PORTER, H. B. Jr. The Ordination Prayers of the Ancient Western Churches. pp. xvii, 98, SPCK; 1967.

Material on the ancient rites of ordination is not easily obtainable; thus this convenient volume of ordination prayers, giving both the critical Latin text and an English translation, is a most welcome work for both specialists and students. An Introduction deals with the Development of the Ancient Rites of Ordination, the Interpretation of the Rites, and the Texts of the Prayers. The Ordination rites of the *Apostolic Tradition*, and the Ordination Prayers of Rome, Gaul, Spain, and England are followed by a chapter on the Later Composite Rites. Introductory comments, annotations, critical notes, bibliography, and index add to the value of the work and aid further research.

L WILLIS, G. G. Further Essays in Early Roman Liturgy. pp. xi, 267, 1 ill., SPCK; 1968.

While this volume contains only five essays the pagination is nearly double that of Willis' previous collection of *Essays in Early Roman Liturgy*, Alcuin Collection XLVI. 'Roman Stational Liturgy' is the title of the first and longest of the essays and covers the Papal Liturgy, Roman Stations and Stational Churches, and the influence of Stations on the Liturgy. The variable prayers of the Roman Mass, the Consecration of Churches down to the 9th Century, St Gregory the Great and the Lord's Prayer in the Roman Mass, and the Early English Liturgy from Augustine to Alcuin, are the subjects dealt with in the remaining four essays. A diagram-map showing the churches of Rome, a list of churches, a full bibliography, and three indexes make up an excellent technical apparatus.

LI FISHER, J. D. C. Christian Initiation: the Reformation Period: Some Early Reformed Rites of Baptism and Confirmation and other Contemporary Documents. pp. ix, 271, SPCK; 1970.

Fisher is undoubtedly a master of his subject. The main object of this second book on Christian Initiation (see Collection XLVII) is to supply an English version of some of the better-known rites of Baptism and Confirmation produced by the Reformers, and a number of documents which help the reader to understand the background and use of these reformed rites. In order to let the documents speak for themselves, editorial comments are brief but, nevertheless, scholarly and packed with detail.

Part I. Baptism, divided into 24 chapters, contains rites and documentation connected with such names as Luther, Osiander, Hermann, Tyndale, Cranmer, Bucer, Calvin, Knox, and Zwingli. Private Baptism is the subject of Part II. which contains the Brandenburg-Nuremberg Order of 1533, Saxon Church Order 1539, Hermann's *Consultation*, the Prayer Book of 1549, the Missale Mixtum, and the Gallicanum. The section on Confirmation contains many of the names mentioned in Part I, plus other interesting and not generally known rites and documentation. A bibliography and two indexes complete the book which will, no doubt, remain a standard work for some time to come.

LII JAGGER, PETER J. Christian Initiation 1552-1969: Rites of Baptism and Confirmation since the Reformation Period. pp. xix, 321, SPCK; 1970.

This volume completes an Alcuin trilogy on the subject of Christian initiation, made up of Collections XLII, LI, LII, which together cover the subject from the first century to the twentieth. Thirty-seven Anglican rites and thirty-four non-

53

Anglican rites are included in this work, each chapter having a short introduction, and in all cases the introductory rubrics of the services, being of theological and liturgical importance, are printed in full. The work is international and ecumenical in scope, containing Anglican rites from England, Ireland, Scotland, Wales, Canada, America, India, Pakistan, Burma and Ceylon, South Africa, West Indies, and Australia. Apart from the appendix, which contains rites from the Philippines, South India and East Africa, the non-Anglican rites are confined to those used in England in the Methodist, Congregationalist, Church of Scotland, Presbyterian, Baptist, Moravian, Lutheran, and Roman Catholic churches. The non-Anglican section also includes the rites of the Book of Common Order 1611, Genevan Service Book 1556, and the Westminster Directory of 1644, which are included because of their historic interest and value. The rites are set out in chronological order, and, with the aid of a full contents-list and numbered texts, ease of reference and cross-reference is achieved.

LIII BRADSHAW, PAUL F. The Anglican Ordinal: Its History and Development from the Reformation to the Present Day. pp. xv, 234, SPCK; 1971.

Countless works have been published on the Anglican Ordinal and Anglican Orders but most of these have been of a polemical nature. The present work is an objective attempt to examine the various rites used and proposed in the Anglican Communion, the reasons for the changes made, and the objections raised against the rites and proposed revisions. Believing that Cranmer was the real author of the Ordinal, Bradshaw rightly feels that it cannot be studied in isolation from what Cranmer believed about Ordination. He therefore examines (in chapters one and two) the influence of Cranmer on the Ordinal and his debt to Bucer and Erasmus. The Puritans and the Ordinal during the period 1550-1602 are studied in the next two chapters showing the effect of the rites of Geneva and John à Lasco on the Puritan and Scottish ordination services. A chapter on Roman Catholics and the Ordinal, 1553-1662, is followed by one on the revision of 1662, where the contributions of Wren, Cosin, and Sancroft, are dealt with. After four well-documented chapters covering Attempts at Revision 1700-1900, Roman Catholics and the Ordinal 1662-1896 and since 1896, and revision in the 20th century, there are two chapters on, 'The Ordinal and reunion', dealing with Ordination and Unification rites, which are a valuable contribution to the study of ecumenism. A seventeen-page bibliography and a four-page index complete the work.

LIV FAWCETT, TIMOTHY J. The Liturgy of Comprehension 1689: An abortive attempt to revise The Book of Common Prayer. pp. xii, 287, Mayhew-McCrimmon; 1973.

This scholarly and well-documented work also helps to throw new light on to the history of the Book of Common Prayer, by showing what at least some 17th-century churchmen felt about 'the incomparable Liturgy' of 1662. One of the avowed aims of William III, on his accession to the English throne, was to draw together the 'Church of England and all Protestant Dissenters'. His attempt to bring about such a reconciliation was the main purpose behind the issue of the Royal Commission on September 17th, 1689. Dr Fawcett's book makes available an accurate working text of the Proposals of the Commissioners who in 1689 attempted to produce what would have been a unique revision of the

Book of Common Prayer. This official but unsuccessful revision was a genuine attempt to alter the Prayer Book in such a way as to make it acceptable to the growing number of Dissenters and thus enable them to return to the Established Church. Based upon manuscripts held at Lambeth Palace Library, the book provides both liturgical scholars and students with liturgical material generally unknown and not easily accessible. An erudite Introduction, select bibliography, and index, in addition to the textual material, help to make this an important work of reference.

LV WHITAKER, E. C. Martin Bucer and The Book of Common Prayer. pp. 183, Mayhew-McCrimmon; 1974.

Whilst the extent of Martin Bucer's influence upon the Prayer Book of 1552 is a matter of some debate, nevertheless he does have a very real place in the history of the Book of Common Prayer. In what is commonly known as the *Censura*, Bucer made a careful study of the first English Prayer Book of 1549. An edition of the work printed in Basle in 1577 is full of errors and obviously produced from a manuscript of very poor quality. Two manuscripts of the *Censura* are available, one at Cambridge in Bucer's own poor handwriting, which contains many deletions and additions. The other is preserved in the Bodleian Library, Oxford. This is beautifully and clearly written by Bucer's amanuensis. The few mistakes have been corrected by Bucer, and the manuscript is signed by him. It is this latter manuscript that Whitaker here reproduces, with the addition of some variant readings from the Cambridge manuscript. In addition to this Latin text, previously inaccessible to most students, we have a good English translation. Also reproduced is the treatise *De Ordinatione Legitima*.

LVI GUSMER, CHARLES W. The Ministry of Healing in the Church of England: An Ecumenical-Liturgical Study. pp. 181, Mayhew-McCrimmon; 1974.

The ministry of healing has a long history within the Christian Church and in more recent years has become a subject of much discussion and investigation. Unfortunately, works of scholarship in this area are somewhat meagre, and thus Dr Gusmer's very interesting and valuable work, originally produced as a doctoral dissertation, is a most welcome contribution to this important, albeit neglected, field. Ecumenical in its perspective, this book, written by a Roman Catholic liturgical scholar, contains four main chapters covering (i) The growth and development of the ministry of healing in the Church of England; (ii) The Anglican understanding of healing; (iii) The Prayer Book and Healing; (iv) Unction of the sick and the laying-on of hands in the Church of England today. The concluding chapter examines the ecumenical possibilities which present themselves on the basis of recent developments in the Roman Catholic theology and liturgy of the sacrament of anointing of the sick. A useful working bibliography and brief index add to the value of the book.

LVII McKENNA, JOHN H. Eucharist and Holy Spirit: The Eucharistic Epiclesis in Twentieth Century Theology. pp. 275, Mayhew-McCrimmon; 1975.

An important contribution to eucharistic theology, with implications well beyond the limits of the title. The first part of the book sets out the patristic evidence, first from the early liturgies and then from the writings of the Fathers, ending with a discussion of the problem of the 'moment of consecration'. Part Two surveys the treatment of the epiclesis by twentieth-century theologians; and Part Three attempts a synthesis. In the latter, great weight is placed upon the part of the 'assembly' in praying, believing, and partaking. This approach opens up new possibilities for ecumenical agreement on eucharistic doctrine. Good bibliography.

LVIII BUXTON, RICHARD F. Eucharist and Institution Narrative: A study in the Roman and Anglican traditions of the Consecration of the Eucharist from the Eighth to the Twentieth Centuries. pp. 276, SPCK; 1976.

Another new approach to eucharistic theology, admirably complementing McKenna's work (LVII, above). Starting from an examination of the provision for further consecration when the consecrated elements have run out, as made in the various Anglican prayer-books (it is a purely Anglican problem), the author rightly uses this as a sort of litmus-test for the theology of consecration underlying the rite concerned. This leads him to a study of seventeenth-century divines from which a general consensus emerges of the need for prayer, validated by recitation of the institution narrative. The limited sense attached to the word 'consecration' in the seventeenth century also becomes very clear. An excellent antidote to the Tractarian interpretation of the Caroline divines.

LIX ROWELL, D. GEOFFREY. The Liturgy of Christian Burial: An Introductory Survey of the Historical Development of Christian Burial Rites. pp. 137, SPCK; 1977.

Starting with Jewish and pagan practice, the author surveys burial rites through the centuries down to the *Alternative Service Book*, then still known as Series 3. A chapter is devoted to Eastern rites, including such little-known examples as the Armenian, Coptic, Ethiopian, and Assyrian. As the subtitle suggests, this is an introduction to the subject rather than an exhaustive treatment; but in view of the almost total absence of works in English dealing with the subject, it is an extremely useful contribution to liturgical study.

This Collection is the first to have an illustration on the cover, an innovation which has continued up to the time of publication of this bibliography.

LX FISHER, JOHN D. C. Confirmation Then and Now. pp. 173, SPCK; 1978.

Since the 1940s, the relation between baptism and confirmation has been a constant subject of controversy. A series of reports and learned studies culminated in the Ely Report of 1971. Canon Fisher sets out to contest the findings of that report. He distinguishes the Catholic view that confirmation is 'in essence a rite for the imparting of the gift of the Holy Spirit' from the Reformed view of it as 'the occasion for personal confession of the faith'. He carefully sets out the patristic evidence, and ends with a survey of the modern debate. He recommends reuniting the laying-on of hands with baptism, and administering the renewal of baptismal promises at the age of responsibility. This study, with its clear relevance to one of the central contemporary liturgical problems, maintains the high standard set by the author's previous Collections (nos. XLVII and LI above).

LXI PORTER, H. BOONE. Jeremy Taylor, Liturgist (1613-1667). pp. 185, SPCK; 1979.

A distinguished American liturgist offers a study of the liturgical work of one of the greatest of the Caroline divines. Jeremy Taylor was such a prolific author in so many different fields that his contribution to liturgy has been given less than its fair share of attention. Yet by his study and adaptation of early Eastern liturgies (including, for example, the Ethiopian), he blazed a trail which led through the Scottish communion office of 1764 and the South Indian of 1947 to the *Alternative Service Book 1980.* The author works through the various services required by the Church of England liturgy, showing how Taylor provided for them in his *Collection of Offices* (1658) and other works. Taylor's baptism service is reproduced in full in facsimile. This erudite study deals with Taylor's theology as well as his forms of service. A photograph of Taylor's church in Northern Ireland adorns the cover.

LXII PERHAM, MICHAEL F. The Communion of Saints: An examination of the place of the Christian dead in the belief, worship, and calendars of the Church. pp. 177, SPCK; 1980.

The author's treatment is mainly historical: starting with the early centuries, he then looks at the Middle Ages, the Reformation, the rise of the *via media*, and the calendar of the 1928 Prayer Book. An important chapter considers the theological issues involved in commemorating the departed, a controversial subject in the Church of England; and especially in singling out some of them for special forms of commemoration. The last chapter deals, not uncritically, with the new Roman Catholic, Church of England, and American Episcopalian calendars. A fresh and readable treatment of one of the most awkward problems facing modern revisers of the liturgy.

LXIII BRADSHAW, PAUL F. Daily Prayer in the Early Church: A Study of the Origin and Early Development of the Divine Office. pp. 191, SPCK; 1981.

Little had appeared in English on the Daily Office since C. W. Dugmore's book some forty years earlier (XLV, above). On the other hand, a good deal of work had been done on the Continent by such scholars as Juan Mateos and Gabriele Winkler. Dr Bradshaw surveys the important Jewish evidence afresh, and the scanty information that we have about the first three Christian centuries. He then goes on to give the first detailed account in English of the distinction between the newly-recognized 'Cathedral office' and the familiar monastic office, as it applies both in the East and in the West. Besides presenting this new picture of the early office as drawn by continental scholars, Dr Bradshaw has a number of suggestions of his own to make, and a number of corrections to Dugmore's account. This will be a standard work of reference for many years.

LXIV STEVENSON, KENNETH W. Nuptial Blessing: A Study of Christian Marriage Rites. pp. 258, SPCK; 1982.

A pioneering survey of marriage services from Old Testament times down to modern Roman Catholic, Anglican, and Free Church rites. The recent work of continental scholars on local medieval uses is utilized, for the first time in English, and carried further. Due attention is given to the Orthodox marriage service, which has been little studied in England. A mass of information is assembled which cannot easily be found elsewhere, and the theology of the various rites is interestingly explored. Ten specimen marriage blessings are printed as an appendix. An invaluable introduction to a subject hitherto totally neglected by the Club.

LXV CUMING, GEOFFREY J. The Godly Order: Texts and Studies relating to the Book of Common Prayer. pp. 200, SPCK; 1983.

A collection of papers, some new, some reprinted. The new ones mostly arise from the writing of the author's *History of Anglican Liturgy* (2nd ed., 1980), and deal with 'topics which needed investigation in greater depth . . . and treatment at greater length' than a textbook allowed. They include a translation of Cranmer's manuscript Daily Offices; the text of the Prayer Book canticles as they appeared in earlier publications; and a discussion of Cranmer's work on the collects. Longer essays on Hermann's *Consultation* and the Anglicanism of John Cosin, together with a study of the sources of the 1549 Canon form the heart of the book, which ends with a short account of the debates on Prayer Book revision in the Convocation of 1908.

LXVI BUCHANAN, COLIN O. Ed. Latest Anglican Liturgies 1976-1984. pp. 278 + folder, SPCK; 1985.

A sequel to the volumes *Modern Anglican Liturgies* (OUP, 1968) and *Further Anglican Liturgies* (Grove, 1975) by the same editor, and uniform with them except that restrictions on space have led to the regrettable omission of the informative introductions which were a feature of the earlier volumes. This volume includes 25 complete communion services from different parts of the Anglican Communion which appeared in the nine years indicated in the title. Comparison with each other and with earlier services is facilitated by presenting them all in accordance with the conventions observed in the previous volumes. An invaluable work of reference covering a period when most churches were achieving some degree of liturgical stability, while others entered the field of revision for the first time.

LXVII BURNISH, RAYMOND F. G. The Meaning of Baptism: A Comparison of the Teaching and Practice of the Fourth Century with the Present Day. pp. 240, SPCK; 1985.

The well-researched book falls into two parts: the first discusses the practice of and teaching on baptism set out in the *catecheses* of Cyril of Jerusalem, John Chrysostom, Theodore of Mopsuestia, and Ambrose. In the second part, the current Orthodox, Roman Catholic, and Baptist rites are handled in the same way. Finally, contemporary teaching in these three communions is compared, and all are set against the fourth-century material. Particular interest is given to the discussion by the fact that the author himself is a Baptist minister, who approaches the material from a different angle than would a Roman or Anglican scholar.

LXVIII GRAY, DONALD C. Earth and Altar: The Evolution of the Parish Communion in the Church of England to 1945. pp. 288, Canterbury Press, Norwich; 1986.

The introduction of the Parish Communion is one of the great liturgical events of this century, and much has been written about its practice. The time was ripe for an examination of its antecedents. After looking at and rejecting Robert Owen's socialism and the Oxford Movement's stress on communion as two possible sources, Dr Gray turns to F. D. Maurice and his heirs, the Christian Socialists, and shows clearly how they stressed the centrality of the eucharist and the desirability of regular communion. The various organizations into which they divided are described in detail, and the personalities involved are vividly drawn. Finally, the service itself and the *Parish and People* movement are shown as the natural outcome of the Christian Socialists' pioneer work. This study breaks new ground, and deserves the attention of social historians as well as of liturgists.

PART III

THE ALCUIN TRACTS
I to XXXVI

I MICKLETHWAITE, J. T. The Ornaments of the Rubric. pp. 80, Longmans, Green; 1897.
This was the very first Alcuin Publication. It was written during a period of controversy when the 'Ritualists' were drawing out the implications of the Ornaments Rubric. Seven meetings of the Alcuin Committee were devoted to the consideration of this publication, every sentence being carefully examined. The work contains a host of details and a very useful index.

II NEWBOLT, W. C. E. Consolidation. pp. 12, Longmans, Green; 1897.
'Consolidation' reproduces an address delivered by Canon Newbolt before the Annual Meeting of the English Church Union on June 1st, 1897. The Catholic Movement, Ritualism, and Ceremonial, all controversial subjects in the late 19th century, are looked at, giving insight into the events of the time.

III LACEY, T. A. Liturgical Interpolations. pp. 21, Longmans, Green; 1898.

Ritual and ceremonial supplementation of the Prayer Book 'Order of Holy Communion' from other sources was the cause of much anxiety to loyal Anglicans of the 19th century. Behind these interpolations lay the 'newly discovered theology of Consecration' with the emphasis upon Sacrifice. This brief work is a record of the situation and practice concerning these matters in the 1890s.

IV ATCHLEY, E. G. CUTHBERT F. The Parish Clerk and his right to read the Liturgical Epistle. pp. viii, 29, Longmans, Green; 1903.

The Eucharist is a corporate act of worship in which every member should take an active part. Reading the Epistle is something that the layman can rightfully do. Drawing evidence from many sources and over many centuries, Atchley supports his theory that the parish clerk has always been an ordained clerk, and has had the right to read the Liturgical Epistle, and this right can now be performed by the lay parish clerk.

V The First English Ordo: A Celebration of the Lord's Supper with One Minister, described and discussed by some members of the Alcuin. Club. pp. 31, Longmans, Green; 1905.

The lack of a satisfactory English *Ordo* giving instruction as to how the priest ought to celebrate the Liturgy resulted in this publication. It is not meant to be an 'Official Alcuin Manual', but describes in detail the ceremonial of the Liturgy in one particular church. Correct ceremonial principles are put forward, rather than an exhaustive attempt to cover every detail.

VI ATCHLEY, E. G. CUTHBERT F. The People's Prayers: Being some considerations on the use of the Litany in Public Worship. pp. 43, Longmans, Green; 1906.

The sub-title of this work is sufficient to indicate that it deals with a much neglected subject. Details of the due liturgical position and the traditional method of rendering the Litany are the main themes of the book.

VII BERESFORD-COOKE, ERNEST. The Sign of the Cross in the Western Liturgies. pp. iv, 32, Longmans, Green; 1907.

While no claim is made that this is a complete examination of the subject, nevertheless it is a very thorough investigation into the use of the Sign of the Cross in the Western Liturgies, and especially its use in the Canon of the Mass. Making the use and purpose of this sacred sign more intelligible is the main objective of the work.

VIII KENNEDY, W. M. The 'Interpretations' of the Bishops and their Influence on the Elizabethan Policy (with an appendix of the original documents). pp. 43, Longmans, Green; 1908.

The documents dealt with in this tract undoubtedly influenced the thoughts of Archbishop Parker and his brethren. It represents a kind of mutual basis for the episcopal policy in the Elizabethan period. Three manuscript copies of the 'Interpretations' are reproduced, and the contents of the documents, which include such subjects as the Royal Injunctions of 1559, the Prayer Book, Burial, and Matrimony, are examined.

IX RILEY, ATHELSTAN. Ed. Prayer Book Revision: the Irreducible Minimum of the Hickleton Conference, showing the proposed rearrangement of the Order for the Holy Communion together with further suggestions, edited with an Introduction, Notes, and an Appendix containing the Canons or Anaphoras of other rites. pp. 59, Mowbray; 1911.

Apart from one chapter on 'The Form for Unction of the Sick', this work is devoted to the Holy Communion. A brief introduction on Prayer Book Revision is followed by a proposed order for the Holy Communion, Collect, Epistle and Gospel at the Burial of the Dead, and a tabular comparison of the Canons of St John Chrysostom, the Roman Church, the 1549 BCP, and the American Prayer Book.

X WOOLLEY, REGINALD MAXWELL. The Bread of the Eucharist. pp. viii, 79, 9 ill., Mowbray; 1913.

This specialized work draws together material from numerous churches including the East and West Syrian, Greek and Russian Orthodox, Coptic, Ethiopian, and Armenian, to say nothing of those of Western Christendom. The Uses of the Church before the Great Schism are examined. The East-West controversy, the Eastern Churches' Uses and certain Eastern Documents, along with the situation in England are also covered in this short but scholarly work. A short index is included.

XI WYATT, E. G. P. English or Roman Use? pp. 14, Mowbray; 1913.

The 'English Use' is a convenient title to express what is aimed at by those who desire loyally to follow the directions given or implied by the Church of England, in the BCP, in respect of Church Ornaments and Ceremonial. This work makes a reasoned plea for the 'English Use' and examines the objections raised against in.

XII FRERE, WALTER HOWARD. Ed. Translated by BARNES, WILFRED J., Russian Observations upon the American Prayer Book. pp. vii, 35, Mowbray; 1917.

These 'Observations' were first published as a report of the Holy Synod in 1904, and are primarily criticisms on the American Prayer Book and its suitability for Orthodox use. While what is said is open to some criticism and reflects the situation at the time of writing, nevertheless the observations on the Holy Communion, Ordination, Baptism, Confirmation, Matrimony, and Penance are practical in character and brotherly in their spirit.

XIII ALCUIN CLUB. A Directory of Ceremonial: Part I. pp. v, 68, 1 ill., Mowbray; 1921.

Produced as an attempt to meet many requests for a simple guide to public worship, this little book is firmly based on the rites and rubrical directions of the BCP. Being of a practical nature, the tract contains little reference to the authorities behind its recommendations. Useful information is given on the church, its furniture, some customs, and the ornaments of the minister. Ceremonial details are given on all Prayer Book services, apart from the rites of ordination. A number of revisions of this work have been published in order to keep in line with liturgical renewal.

XIV Ceremonial Pictured in Photographs: A companion volume to the 'Directory of Ceremonial' (Tract XIII). pp. 43, 18 ill., Mowbray; 1924.

With the help of fourteen well-produced photographs the

main ceremonial actions of the Solemn Eucharist are clearly illustrated. Each photograph is accompanied by an explanatory note, further elucidation being obtainable in the 'Directory'. Two of the remaining photographs serve to illustrate Solemn Mattins or Evensong.

XV BISHOP, W. C, ed. FELTOE, C. L. The Mozarabic and Ambrosian Rites: Four Essays in Comparative Liturgiology. pp. vi, 134, Mowbray; 1924.

W. C. Bishop (1854-1922) was a man of great learning and sound scholarship who continued his liturgical research until nearly the end of his life. His actual output of work was exceedingly small, but its quality very high. These four essays, previously published in article form, are excellent specimens as to the method and depth of his research, and examine The Occasional Offices in Spain, The Mass in Spain, The Breviary in Spain, and the Breviary at Milan.

XVI GASELEE, Sir STEPHEN. The Uniats and their Rites. pp. 16, 3 ill., Mowbray; 1925.

The contents of this tract were read as a paper before a meeting of the Alcuin Club on November 20th, 1924. There is very little about the actual Uniat rites and, as one would expect from a paper, the breadth and depth are somewhat limited. Nevertheless, it is a useful, albeit brief, introduction to the subject. Eight illustrations of Uniat Eucharistic dress, and one of a priest in out-door dress, are given on the three illustrated pages.

XVII DEARMER, PERCY. Linen Ornaments of the Church. pp. 26, 7 ill., OUP; 1929.

A useful little work of practical rather than scholarly nature. Linen ornaments, lawfully used in the Anglican Communion, are summed up by the author under four headings: Lesser cloths etc., the Lenten Array, Linen for the Lord's Table, Linen for Vessels; and details of their use, size, and upkeep are given.

XVIII CLAYTON, H. J. Cassock and Gown. pp. 16, 6 ill., OUP; 1929.

The dress of the clergy, says Clayton, is 'at all times of their ministration' regulated by the Ornaments Rubric, while their out-of-door dress is regulated by Canon 74 of 1603-04. In order to understand the Canon the author examines the walking dress of the clergy before the Reformation. Almost the entire work is devoted to the use of the Gown.

XIX ALCUIN CLUB: A Directory of Ceremonial: Part II. pp. v, 56, 6 ill., OUP; 1930.

This tract is the sequence to Tract XIII. Its purpose is to make suggestions for the conduct of services on the major fasts and festivals of the Church's year. Directions and ceremonial details are based upon the practices of some English Cathedrals during the Middle Ages. They are put forward as suggestions for enriching the services of the BCP. The work, which was last revised in 1965, offers a very useful guide based on sound liturgical principles and the 'English Use'.

XX DUNLOP, COLIN. Processions: A dissertation together with practical suggestions. pp. 79, 4 ill., OUP; 1932.

Historic practice and sound liturgical principles, tinged with common sense, lay behind the suggestions made as to the use and development of Processions today. Practical and useful details on various aspects connected with Processions are given, e.g. Order, Banners, Music, Dress, Stations, along with a number of suggested schemes. While dated in places, this tract is still a very useful manual on the subject.

XXI A Server's Manual for the Holy Communion. pp. 30, 1 ill., Mowbray; 1935.

Making good servers is the aim of this practical manual. Directions are based upon the 1662 rite with the allowable variations of the proposed rite of 1928. The rite is printed in full with the instructions inserted where necessary. Two revisions of this manual have been published, the first in 1940, and the second in 1965, by G. B. Timms.

XXII ARNOLD, J. H. Ed. Anglican Liturgies. pp. x, 195, OUP; 1939.

Beginning with the English Rite of 1662, Arnold provides a collection of seven Eucharistic rites. The rites reproduced are: the English rites of 1662 and 1928, Scottish Liturgy (1929), American Rite (1928), South African (1929), Indian Liturgy (1933), and the Ceylon Liturgy (1938). Three appendixes by W. H. Frere are also included: Deviations of the Irish rite from the English 1662; Deviations of the Canadian rite from the English 1662; An Essay in Liturgical Constructions.

XXIII MORISON, STANLEY. English Prayer Books: An introduction to the literature of Christian Public Worship. pp. viii, 143, OUP; 1943.

In this small but detailed work, Morison describes the origin and development of the existing service books normally used in the churches of England. Three chapters on the 'Creative Period' cover the Apostolic times to the 15th century. Chapter four, which takes up nearly half the book, covers the Modern Period, 16th-20th centuries, and deals with the various revisions of the BCP, up to 1928. A final chapter examines Free Church adaptations of the BCP, and some forms designed to meet special needs. There is a detailed bibliography and two indexes on authors and printers, and Prayer Books and Literature.

XXIV BATE, HERBERT NEWELL and EELES, FRANCIS C. Thoughts on the shape of the Liturgy. pp. 56, Mowbray; 1946.

Dr H. N. Bate gave a lifetime of research and thought to the early ages of the Church, and in the latter part of his life he turned his attention especially to early liturgy. Two of his careful studies in this sphere are here reproduced: 'Eucharistic Worship – The Primitive Type', and 'On Consecration Prayers'. To these is added a third essay, by Dr F. C. Eeles, 'The Rite of 1662 Re-examined.'

XXV EELES, FRANCIS C. Notes on Episcopal Ornaments and Ceremonial. pp. 38, Mowbray; 1948.

A lack of material and guidance on Anglican Episcopal ceremonial, a growing use of adaptations of Roman ceremonial, and episcopal requests for guidance, resulted in this slender but useful Tract. The ceremonial here prescribed is that of English post-Reformation tradition supplemented, where necessary, by the pontifical ceremonial of the pre-Reformation English Use. While the author acknowledges the need for a much fuller work, what he writes does cover the essential points. After a chapter on 'The Episcopal Ornaments', notes are given on the Consecration of Churches and Altars, Confirmation, Ordination, Consecration of Bishops, Christenings, and Burial. An appendix gives a summary of the use of Episcopal Ornaments.

XXVI BERRY, C. LEO. A Plea for the Prayer of Oblation. pp. 27, Mowbray; 1951.

Berry argues that for four centuries the Church of England has allowed two alternative orders of Holy Communion, a fact generally unrecognized in spite of the considerable doctrinal differences between the two rites. In the 1662 rite the alternatives offered which, Berry maintained, constitute two very different rites are, Order A, Prayer of Consecration plus Prayer of Oblation; Order B, Prayer of Consecration plus Prayer of Thanksgiving. The same alternatives are offered in the revision of 1927-28. For the author, the Catholic ideal is the Prayer of Consecration plus Oblation, the whole act being terminated with the Communion of the people, his main plea being for the inclusion of the Oblation.

XXVII SRAWLEY, JAMES HERBERT. The Liturgical Movement: Its origin and growth. pp. 34, Mowbray; 1954.

Tracing the Liturgical Movement in the Roman Catholic Church from its birth, due to the initiative of Pius X, to the 1950s, Srawley gives a rapid, but fairly detailed, survey of the major events and contributors in a Movement which has been an important feature of the present century. Succinct reviews of the main Roman literary contributions to the Movement enable present readers to appreciate just how far liturgical renewal, with its emphasis upon the Eucharist and lay participation, had advanced since the turn of the century. Srawley concludes with five points showing how some of these reforms and suggested reforms are parallel with earlier changes which began in England in 1549.

XXVIII BRITTAIN, F. Latin in Church: The History of its pronunciation. pp. 98, Mowbray; 1955.

The object of this unique little book is to trace the history of the pronunciation of Latin in post-classical times, particularly in ecclesiastical usage. In the first edition of this work, published in 1934, the writer showed (i) that the pronunciation of ecclesiastical Latin throughout the ages has not differed essentially from the pronunciation of secular Latin; (ii) that Latin, both ecclesiastical and secular, has normally been pronounced in each country (including England) on the same principles as the vernacular; (iii) that the Reformation of the 16th century caused no change in the pronunciation of Latin, either ecclesiastical or secular. Brittain's subsequent research, during the 20 years following the first edition, confirmed each of his earlier conclusions. In this new edition much new material is incorporated. There is also a brief index.

XXIX POCKNEE, CYRIL E. The French Diocesan Hymns and Their Melodies. pp. vi, 162, Faith Press; 1954.

During the reign of Louis XIV some of the refined and scholarly leaders of the French Church criticised both the matter and manner of the existing Breviary Offices. But their criticism was objective and constructive and led to what was termed the 'Neo-Gallican' Breviaries and Missals. This tract is concerned only with the hymnological aspects of these books. Many of the hymns they included have now passed, in translated form, into the hymnals of the English Church. In this pioneer work Pocknee gives five chapters covering the Historical Background, the Hymns and their writers, the Hymn Melodies, Musical Illustrations, and Texts and Translations. A bibliography and two indexes are also included.

XXX POCKNEE, CYRIL E. Liturgical Vesture: Its Origins and Development. pp. 57, 15 ill., Mowbray; 1960.

This book provides a very readable and well documented introduction to the common origin and development of liturgical vestments and insignia, as used in the main branches of Christendom, with special emphasis upon Eucharistic vestments. There are chapters on the Amice, Maniple or Fanon, Stole, Albe, Chasuble and Cope, Dalmatic and Tunicle, and the Surplice. The longest chapter is on Episcopal Insignia and deals with the Mitre, Crozier, Ring, Pectoral Cross, and the Pallium. A final chapter covers the Christian Altar and its Vesture. An appendix dealing with the sizes of various items of vesture and a select bibliography, complete the work.

XXXI COWLEY, PATRICK. Advent: its liturgical significance. pp. 88, Faith Press; 1960.

What is the true meaning of Advent? This is the question which Patrick Cowley seeks to answer in the course of this book. He believes that there is much confusion and misunderstanding as to the meaning of Advent. Thus it is seen either as the beginning of the Christian Year, or as a preparation for Christmas Day. But, as he points out, the real meaning and liturgical significance are concerned with the end of the Church's year, even with the end of all time. After an introductory chapter on the Sacred Calendar, he has five chapters entitled 'Advent and': Advent and Lent, and Christmas, and the Church's New Year, and 'Excita', and its Distortions, with the final chapter on The Decline of Advent. Nine appendixes and a bibliography complete the work.

XXXII POCKNEE, CYRIL E. Cross and Crucifix: In Christian Worship and Devotion. pp. 78, 35 ill., Mowbray; 1962.

While there are a number of monographs, in English, which deal with certain aspects of the Cross and Crucifix, this work seeks to provide a brief but general survey of the use of the Cross in Christian worship and devotion. Thirty-five beautiful plates, with brief notes, give valuable illustrations to the six chapters on the Sign of the Cross, the Advent of the Crucifix, Towards Realism, the Rood and its Crucifix, Pectoral and Reliquary Crosses, and the Processional and Altar Crosses.

XXXIII POCKNEE, CYRIL E. The Christian Altar: In History and Today. pp. 112, 35 ill., Mowbray; 1963.

This carefully documented and well illustrated work offers the English reader a full-scale study of the development of the Altar in Christian worship. Scholarly and well supported by countless references to authoritative sources, which offer many opportunities for further research, the book is easy reading. Beginning with the Lord's Table, Pocknee moves on to examine: Side Altars and their multiplication, the Altar Canopy and its Veils, Altar Screens, Orientation at Prayer and the Position of the Celebrant at the Altar, and the Hanging Pyx. A final chapter gives some practical considerations in the design of an Altar. There is a select bibliography and a short index.

XXXIV RAMSEY, MICHAEL and others. The English Prayer Book 1549-1662. pp. 114, SPCK; 1963.

To mark the Tercentenary of the 1662 BCP, a series of

lectures were delivered in the Library of Lambeth Palace. These lectures, and a sermon by the Archbishop of Canterbury, are reprinted in this tract. Professor Dugmore's lecture deals with the first 10 years of the Prayer Book's history, 1549-59. The Problem of Uniformity, 1559-1604, is covered by Dr T. M. Parker. Puritan Alternatives to the BCP, in the form of *The Directory* and Richard Baxter's *Reformed Liturgy*, are considered by Professor E. C. Ratcliff. The process of revision, which resulted in the Book annexed to the Act of Uniformity of 1662, is skilfully dealt with by Dr G. J. Cuming.

XXXV JONES, C. P. M. Ed., A Manual for Holy Week. pp. x, 209, SPCK; 1967.

Twenty writers have made contributions of varying lengths to this most useful manual. Contents are wide ranging, some being scholarly, but most are practical. Amongst the subjects considered are The Origins of Holy Week, Holy Week in the Orthodox Church, the Anglican Tradition, Holy Week in the life of the Parish, Drama for Passiontide, Audio-visual Aid, Children and Holy Week. A useful bibliography and a good index add to the value of a book which most parish priests would find to be a mine of information on the subject.

XXXVI COWLEY, PATRICK. The Church Houses: Their religious and social significance. pp. 99, SPCK; 1970.

The little-known and much-neglected subject of Church Houses is here skilfully dealt with and presented in a most fascinating way. These houses were erected for 'church ales', or parish parties which were held at special festivals. Supporting this work with much unpublished material, Cowley surveys the subject from the first appearance of the houses c.1450 to their decline and virtual disappearance c.1630.

77

PART IV

THE ALCUIN PAMPHLETS
I to XIX

I LACEY, T. A. Liturgical Interpolations and Prayer Book Revision. pp. 34, Mowbray; 1912.

With this pamphlet began the Alcuin series of 'Prayer Book Revision Pamphlets'. Attached to this first pamphlet was a note by the Alcuin Committee stating that, while the Alcuin Club took 'no side in the discussion as to the advisability at this time of Prayer Book Revision', it could help to spread 'sound knowledge upon liturgical subjects, and the consequent growth in the mind of the English Church of a high and consistent ideal of worship.' Throughout its history the Club has done just this, and in this series of pamphlets it made a valuable contribution to Prayer Book Revision.

This first pamphlet offered a new and enlarged edition of the well received Alcuin Tract III, of 1898. The continuing practice of the interpolation of Roman material in the use of the Prayer Book seemed to demand a reprint of this work.

II FRERE, W. H. The Liturgical Gospels. pp. viii, 48, Mowbray; 1913.

Frere's study of Latin Gospel-books led him to offer his conclusions for the purpose of the improvement of the series of Liturgical Gospels provided in the Prayer Book. His detailed study in this field is contained in Collections XXVIII, XXX, XXXII. Having considered the subject of the enrichment of the Gospel-lections in the BCP, Frere gives a brief, but very well documented survey covering the Christian Year and other related subjects.

III BAYLAY, ATWELL M. Y. A Century of Collects: selected and translated. pp. 42, Mowbray; 1913.

Both 'Roman' and 'Gallican' types of Collects are provided in this collection. Alongside the Latin originals are given English translations. There are Collects for the various seasons of the Church's year, plus Collects for a variety of festivals and occasions; on the whole, an interesting and still useful little collection of ancient prayers.

IV STALEY, VERNON. The Manual Acts: prescribed in the rubrics of the Prayer of Consecration of the Eucharist, according to the Anglican Rite. pp. 25, Mowbray; 1913.

A careful examination of the directions accompanying the Prayer of Consecration in the Communion Service of 1662, and criticism of them, is the object of this pamphlet. The author believes that a comparison of these directions with those of the 1549 BCP, and with due comparison of Catholic precedent, show how far the developments which are evident in the 1662 rite have moved along wrong and undesirable lines. He goes on to offer suggestions which, he believes, are more accurate and expressive of the Eucharistic act. An appendix deals with the 'Symbolical Fraction of the Bread'.

V WYATT, E. G. P. The Eucharistic Prayer. pp. 64, Mowbray; 1914.

There is, says Wyatt, a general agreement that the Eucharistic Prayer of the BCP is defective and ill arranged. Thus there is need for its revision. The purpose of this pamphlet is to examine whether this revision should take the direction of approximation to the Roman Canon or not. In order to answer this question, he carefully examines the Canon of the Roman Rite and from this examination draws his conclusions.

VI Memorial Services. pp. 27, Mowbray; 1914.

The contents of this small pamphlet are extracted from *A Prayer Book Revised*, issued in 1913, with a preface by the then Bishop of Oxford (Charles Gore). Four services are here reproduced: The Quire Service for the Burial of the Dead, the Commemoration of the Departed, the Dirge, and At the Holy Communion.

VII WYATT, E. G. P. The Burial Service. pp. 23, Mowbray; 1918.

The most unsatisfactory nature of the 1662 BCP Burial Service, which is concerned more with the consolation of the bereaved than with the commendation of the departed to God, leads Wyatt to pose the question: 'How can this unsatisfactory situation be remedied?' He feels that the Burial Service of the 1549 BCP is far superior to that of 1662, but even this has its defects. The Primer of 1559 contains the Dirge. Apart from the extreme length of the service, this, he thinks, offers an excellent memorial service. A compromise is suggested; the Mattins part of the Dirge could be used more or less as it stands in the Primer. To this are added a number of additional items, offering what Wyatt believes is a much more acceptable service. Following his introduction to the subject, his proposed rite is given in full.

VIII FRERE, W. H. The Primitive Consecration Prayer. pp. iii, 26, Mowbray; 1922.

This pamphlet contains the texts of a Lecture given at the Annual Meeting of the Alcuin Club, 1922. The object of the lecture was to examine the Primitive Consecration Prayer found in the *Apostolic Constitutions*, which Frere does in a most interesting and scholarly way, making a small but valuable contribution to research in this particular field.

IX ATCHLEY, CUTHBERT. 'He that readeth the Epistle'. pp. viii, 29, 1 ill., OUP; 1927.

The revised Order of Holy Communion in N.A. 84., included the rubric: 'And immediately after the Collect, he that readeth the Epistle shall say . . . Then the Deacon or Priest that readeth the Gospel . . . shall say.' In view of this proposed rubric the Alcuin Committee felt that Tract IV, which serves as an admirable commentary on this proposed rubric, ought to be re-issued as a cheap pamphlet. Thus this pamphlet was produced, being a reprint, with the addition of one illustration, of Tract IV.

X MURRAY, D. L. Reservation, its Purpose and Method. pp. 36, Mowbray; 1923.

Eucharistic Presence and Sacrifice, and various practices which have evolved in connection with the Reserved Sacrament, are briefly dealt with in the opening pages of this work. Devotion to the Sacrament outside the Eucharistic Liturgy, with reflections on the situation in the English Church, take up the rest of this small but useful pamphlet.

XI DUNLOP, COLIN. What is the English Use? An inquiry into the principles underlying the conduct of Public Worship in the Church of England. pp. 35, Mowbray; 1923.

After looking at the controversy surrounding the 'English Use' and the practice of borrowing from the 'Roman Use', Dunlop gives a Rationale of the English Use followed by a section on 'What the English Use is Not.' Liturgical Authority, the Fitness of the English Use, and Practical Hints, are covered in the remaining chapters. The work reflects very much the times in which it was written.

XII A Survey of the Proposals for the Alternative Prayer Book: Part I, The Order of Holy Communion. pp. 67, Mowbray; 1923.

When this pamphlet was written, three schemes for an Alternative Prayer Book were being considered by the Church of England. There was the official scheme put forward by the Convocations and National Assembly, the Church Union scheme, and a private alternative suggested by the then Bishop of Manchester. The purpose of this pamphlet, produced by a group of members of the Alcuin Club, was to survey what these three schemes proposed regarding the Holy Communion, and to indicate how they could be simplified and combined.

XIII A Survey of the Proposals for the Alternative Prayer Book: Part II, Occasional Offices. pp. 87, Mowbray; 1924.

Pamphlet XII examined suggested Alternatives put forward in three documents for a revised Eucharistic Liturgy; the same documents are examined in this pamphlet, but the survey is extended to the Occasional Offices. Two interesting proposals were put forward by the English Church Union Scheme viz: the use of Chrism and the Chrysom as enrichments of the baptismal rite.

XIV A Survey of the Proposals of the Alternative Prayer Book: Part III, The Calendar &c., the Collects, Epistles and Gospels, and the Ordination Services. pp. 91, Mowbray; 1924.

This pamphlet completes the Alcuin Survey of three proposals for an alternative Prayer Book. The Calendar, Collects, Epistles, and Gospels, and the Ordination Services, are all carefully considered and compared, and suggestions are made.

XV ADDLESHAW, G. W. O. The Early Parochial System and the Divine Office. pp. 32, Mowbray; 1957.

The contents of this pamphlet were delivered as a paper to the 1956 Annual Meeting of the Alcuin Club. The single aim of the author is to consider the place occupied by the public recitation of the divine office in the life of parish churches under the early parochial system. He achieves his aim and leaves the reader in his debt.

XVI JASPER, R. C. D. The Position of the Celebrant at the Eucharist. pp. 26, Mowbray; 1959.

When this essay was first published, the author expressed his opinion that he was providing no more than the briefest introduction to a complicated and somewhat obscure subject. What he said was offered as a guide to further study. It still offers useful guidance on a subject still being debated.

XVII HINCHLIFF, PETER. The South African rite and the 1928 Prayer Book. pp. 21, Mowbray; 1960.

Considerable controversy surrounded the proposed Prayer Book of 1928, which had, to say the least, a very stormy passage. Hinchliff briefly outlines the reasons for the rejection of the 1928 proposed BCP. He sees a complete contrast in the comparatively calm and painless passage of the South African Rite of Holy Communion, which was widely accepted and used within a few years of receiving canonical authority. The reasons for the painless course of revision within South Africa are briefly recorded.

XVIII JASPER, R. C. D. The Search for an Apostolic Liturgy. pp. 30, Mowbray; 1963.

Delivered as a paper to the Annual Meeting of the Alcuin Club, 1961, this pamphlet offers a brief but useful survey of the work of British Scholars on the origins of the Eucharistic Liturgy. A host of names appear, beginning with Herbert Thorndike (1598-1672); the pamphlet is a reminder of how much English scholars have contributed in this field.

XIX STREATFEILD, FRANK. Latin Versions of the Book of Common Prayer. pp. 33, 1 ill., Mowbray; 1964.

A useful bibliography and four appendixes add to the value of this little work. Divided into three parts, it covers Complete Books, Abbreviated Books, and Litanies used in Convocation.

PART V

THE ALCUIN MANUALS
I to III

I PERHAM, MICHAEL F. The Eucharist. pp. 65, SPCK; 1978. 2nd edition: pp. 59, SPCK; 1981.
A discussion of the practical problems of presenting the Eucharist, with particular reference to the *Alternative Service Book*, and some new ideas.

II BRADSHAW, PAUL F. and JENNINGS, ROBERT C. Episcopal Services. pp. 31, SPCK & CLA; 1980.
What a bishop should wear and do in church services. Published jointly with the Church Literature Association. Full instructions on how to make a pair of *vimpe*.

III STEVENSON, KENNETH W. Family Services. pp. 45, SPCK; 1981.
Chapter-headings: Aims, Ingredients, Presentation, Resources, Samples. An excellent guide for the preparation of informal but not aliturgical services.

(No number) DRAPER, MARTIN P. and TIMMS, GEORGE B. The Cloud of Witnesses. pp. 224, Collins Liturgical Publications; 1982.
Collects (by George Timms), readings (biblical and non-biblical), psalms, and sentences for the Lesser Festivals and Holy Days in the calendar of the *Alternative Service Book*.

PART VI

THE MISCELLANEOUS PUBLICATIONS

DUNCAN-JONES, A. S. Why Change the Communion Service? pp. 22, Mowbray; 1934.
Behind the various revisions of the Eucharistic Liturgy in the Anglican Communion Duncan-Jones sees the parent rite of 1549. He sees the 1552 revision, the immediate predecessor to 1662, as being unsatisfactory. The main defect of the 1552 rite, as retained in 1662, is the inadequacy of the Canon. The Prayer of Consecration is seen to be lacking in that there is no invocation, there is a lack of 'true eucharistic quality', and the absence of an oblation or anamnesis. A further defect is that the service contains no specific prayer for the departed. The proposed Eucharistic Liturgy of 1928 is seen as superior to that of 1662, and as being liturgically and spiritually satisfying. This paper was delivered to the Annual Meeting of the Alcuin Club in December, 1934.

Eucharistic Worship of the Old Catholic Church of the Netherlands, with notes, and translations of the Dutch rites. pp. 36, 1 ill., Society of Willibrord; 1938.
At Bonn, Germany, in July 1931, a joint session of Anglican and Old Catholic Commissions agreed to terms of intercommunion; thus the contents of this little-known pamphlet are important for every Anglican. Introductory chapters cover the terms of the Bonn Agreement, a very brief history of the Old Catholics, the Declaration of Utrecht (1889), Old

Catholic Ceremonial and Music, and notes for Anglicans who wish to receive Holy Communion in Old Catholic Churches. The Common Order of the Holy Service of the Mass according to the use of the Old Catholic Church of the Netherlands is given in full, in English translation.

TIMMS, G. B. Dixit Cranmer: A reply to Dom Gregory. pp. 37, Mowbray; 1946.

Dix's *The Shape of the Liturgy* has been widely acknowledged as one of the most valuable and scholarly Anglican contributions to the field of Eucharistic theology and liturgiology. But the magnitude of the work does not mean that it is beyond criticism. George Timms in this paper, read to the Annual Meeting of the Alcuin Club in 1946, takes issue over one small part of Dix's work. For Timms the point is one of major importance. In chapter sixteen, 'The Reformation and the Anglican Liturgy' Dix expresses his opinion that Cranmer's doctrine of Communion is pure Zwinglianism, and his doctrine of the sacrificial aspect is purely subjective. By allowing Cranmer to speak for himself, Timms endeavours to show how Dix's view of Cranmer's theology is incorrect. He then sets out Cranmer's true Eucharistic theology. While Cranmer's teaching was not free from defects and not always clear, nevertheless, Timms believes, Cranmer knew just where he wanted to stand, theologically, and that was between the extremes of Lutheranism and Zwinglianism.

SMETHURST, A. F. The New Canons and Obedience to the Book of Common Prayer. pp. 15, Mowbray; 1950.

The Act of Uniformity and Canons XIV and XXXVI of 1603, demand of the Anglican Clergy strict uniformity to the service of the 1662 BCP. With the Clerical Subscription Act of 1885, provision was made for certain discretionary powers in liturgical matters to be vested in the Bishop of the Diocese.

In this paper, read before the 1950 Annual Meeting of the Alcuin Club, Smethurst looks at the revision of Canon Law being carried out by the Convocations. He shows how the aim of Canon C XIII is to retain the fundamental requirement of clerical obedience and loyalty to the BCP, while allowing reasonable latitude and opportunity for liturgical experiment and development under proper constitutional control.

MORTIMER, R. C. The Celebrant and Minister of the Eucharist. pp. 40, Mowbray; 1957.

Through the centuries the Church has required that the Minister of the Eucharist shall be a man episcopally ordained. This essay attempts to describe and explain the Church's insistence on this requirement. Five subjects are examined: The Requirement of Ordination, the Celebrant in the Early Church, the Bishop and the Primitive Celebrant, Concelebration, and the Deacon and the Eucharist. A short index is also included.

RABY, F. J. E. The Poetry of the Eucharist. pp. 44, Mowbray; 1957.

Liturgical and other poetry has been associated with the Eucharist from at least the 5th century. Raby's brief essay looks at the subject from early times until the present day. Eastern Liturgical Hymns provide the earliest available material, and these are covered in the first five pages of the work, while the rest of the book is confined to material produced in Western Christendom. Footnotes, a short bibliography, and an index offer the interested reader sufficient material to pursue the subject further.

OAKLEY, AUSTIN. The Orthodox Liturgy. pp. 50, Mowbray; 1958.
This short work is no more than a very brief, albeit useful, introduction to a great and somewhat complicated subject. The Liturgies of SS Basil, Chrysostom, Gregory, and James are briefly introduced, being followed by a section 'The Adjuncts of Orthodox Worship', dealing with the Church, Altar Vessels and Cloths, and Vestments. There are also chapters on The Divine Liturgy, The Religious Significance of the Holy Liturgy, and an appendix, Preparation and Thanksgiving for Holy Communion, plus a short bibliography.

PORTER, W. S. The Gallican Rite. pp. 64, Mowbray; 1958.
Composed of seven brief but well-documented chapters, this study provides a useful introduction to a subject on which there is very little material available to the English reader. First the writer surveys the problems behind the subject. He then looks at the rite, its structure, content, and general characteristics. The final chapter considers the disappearance of the rite. For such a short book, the bibliography and index are excellent.

CLARKE, W. K. LOWTHER. The Alcuin Club, 1897-1961 pp. 4; 1961. A publicity leaflet.

COURATIN, A. H. and TRIPP, D. H. Edward Craddock Ratcliff 1896-1967: A Bibliography of his Published Works. pp. 18; 1972.
This pamphlet contains a short memoir of a great liturgical scholar and a list of all his published works.

Liturgy in the Parish: Alcuin Leaflets. Volume I. pp. 50, 1 ill., Mowbray; (no date).
Six Alcuin Leaflets, all published separately in leaflet form, make up this volume. Praying with the Church, The Consecration of the Eucharist, English Use, The Parish Eucharist, The Catholic Altar, and Processions, are the titles of the leaflets. Produced with the non-expert in mind, and for parish distribution, these leaflets give a brief introduction to a number of important subjects covered in other major Alcuin Publications.

Simple Eucharistic Ceremonial. Alcuin Leaflet No. 7. pp. 8.
This seventh leaflet in the series 'Liturgy in the Parish' deals very briefly with the theme 'How to do what must be done in celebrating the Eucharist – aiming at the bare minimum of ceremony'.

Eucharistic Ceremonial in One-Priest Parishes. Alcuin Leaflet No. 8. pp. 12.
This title is a clear description of the contents of this very practical leaflet.

Worship Today:
1. *The Daily Eucharist.* W. K. Lowther Clarke.
2. *Processions.* J. W. Poole.
3. *The Fast Before Communion.* G. B. Timms.
4. *The Canon.* R. C. D. Jasper.
5. *Why Mattins and Evensong?* W. K. Lowther Clarke.
6. *The Parish Communion.* Martin Pierce.
   12 pages each. No publisher or date given, though they were produced in the early 1960s.

These pamphlets are simply written, and were published with the intention of educating the English Churchman on a number of important liturgical subjects. In each case the title is sufficient to indicate the general contents.

PART VII

ALCUIN CLUB OCCASIONAL JOURNALS

These contain the Annual Reports of the Club and usually also a paper read at the Annual Festival.

1975 CRICHTON, Mgr J. D. The New Roman Mass and the Anglican Series Three.
1977 KEMP, Bishop Eric. The Art of Worship.
1978 BRADSHAW, Paul. The Origins of the Daily Office.
1979 FISHER, J. D. C. The New Rites of Initiation.
1980 DRAPER, M. P. Percy Dearmer and the English Hymnal.
1981 ASB and Supporting Literature: A Guide.
1983 TURNER, Mark. The Liturgy of the Sick.
1984 GRAY, Donald. The Influence of Tractarian Principles on Parish Worship 1839-1849.

INDEX OF AUTHORS

93

INDEX OF SUBJECTS

www.ingramcontent.com/pod-product-compliance
Lightning Source LLC
Chambersburg PA
CBHW071847090426
42811CB00029B/1946